EVERYDAY

Celebrity

A PERSONAL BRANDING GUIDE
FROM A HOLLYWOOD MEDIA COACH

Jess Ponce III

Dedication

This is dedicated to my greatest childhood fan,
Grandma Grace.
Her simple, yet powerful, example as an *everyday celebrity*
helped me and countless others shine.

Contents

Preface

What's in a Name?

I was "that" boy: a pudgy, curly-haired, wide-eyed, seven-year-old, dressed in a parochial school uniform playing alone on an asphalt playground during recess. The other boys in my first-grade class spent their time role-playing *CHiPs*, a popular 1970's U.S. television show about the California Highway Patrol. I wasn't interested. Instead, I created my own imaginary games, inventing unknown superheroes with powers like walking through walls or being invisible. They were not typical superheroes like Batman or Superman.

Awkward and shy, yet vocal and theatrical, I was content dreaming up unique scenarios and ways to entertain myself. After school, my grandmother, who lived across the street from the Catholic church and my elementary school, smiled at my antics. My skits brightened her day and helped her when she was not feeling well. Grandma Grace said, "One day, *mijo*, you will entertain lots of people. It's who you are meant to be."

Her words lifted my spirits.

Shortly after, on one bright, sunny, Southern California afternoon, a group of eighth-grade girls called me over to their side of the playground. They seemed so old to me, a mere first-grader. I was nervous but excited that they somehow knew me.

1

One girl said to me, "What's your name?"

I answered, "Jesse Ponce."

They laughed. It struck me as strange, but I was still giddy from the excitement of being around the big kids. Then another girl asked, "What's your name?"

Again I responded, "Jesse Ponce."

This time they roared even more loudly. Then one final time, another girl asked the same question, "What's your name?"

In horror, I heard someone else answer, "My name is Jes-sss-e Ponc-ssss-e." They all pointed at me and howled yet again.

At that moment, I realized I spoke with a lisp. They were laughing at me.

I was humiliated. I was broken. I felt violated and betrayed. They were the big kids. They were supposed to watch out for the little guys like me. They were supposed to protect us. After all, this was a Catholic school. Why had they done that?

Swallowing my tears, I walked away. That's when I discovered I had a vulnerability that hit me at my core, one that others could exploit. It was the way I talked.

They could make fun of everything else, from how I walked to how I acted. I was used to that. But to make fun of the way I talked was like taking away the air I breathed.

At seven years old, I made a decision. From that day forward, I would do my best to avoid any word with an "s" sound. That meant I had to find creative ways to speak and present myself.

I decided to use my words to help me never be a victim again.

That determination set me on the path I am on today in the world of communication. I found passion and success and reached my career goal as a media professional.

Now my mission goes deeper. It is to help others get over their own fears in communication, help them find their words, stand with certainty, and speak their truth.

The Road from Hollywood

Growing up in Southern California, I didn't have to look too far to find myself in the middle of the media capital of the world. At 23-years-old, however, I was initially awestruck by all the Hollywood glitz and glamor at my first job as a production assistant on the morning news broadcast for a local Los Angeles television station.

In typical Hollywood style, this program wasn't conventional at all. In addition to scheduled interviews, celebrity after celebrity often crashed the set. Film actors, TV stars, high-profile figures, and musicians did the weather and stayed for a part of the show.

Imagine hearing it was going to be a windy Wednesday afternoon from classic Hollywood icons like Little Richard or ZsaZsa Gabor. Former U.S. President Jimmy Carter was charming and engaging—and more interested in knowing about me than talking about himself.

Well-known public figures played and acted with the media like they were in an elaborate dance. Their personalities came alive and it was amazing to watch.

After that first L.A. morning news show, I went on to work for a myriad of talk shows and entertainment newsmagazine programs—and interacted with amazing producers, experts, and celebrities. Growing more comfortable and confident around them, I produced and conducted interviews myself. As my experience grew, I was courted by publicity agencies to coach celebrities. I helped them prepare for press conferences, interviews, and public appearances.

My work as a producer and interviewer allowed me to see the person behind the popular image. I quickly got past being "star struck" (although now and then I can't help it) and dove deep into my passion for breaking down how we talk about ourselves—*the art of self-promotion.*

My media coaching practice expanded outside Hollywood to include TV hosts, experts, and executives. This led to facilitating workshops and creating a coaching program called The A Factor™.

In 2010, my long-time colleague Adora English and I partnered together to launch *Media 2x3*, a media company that develops and packages personality brands.

My sights went international when I met Emily Liu, a leadership consultant and performance coach from Taiwan. She courted me to co-develop a communication workshop, which was ultimately the impetus for this book.

My work and purpose are now global: I'm a media coach who brings out the best in my clients.

It doesn't matter where they are from: Hollywood, another U.S. city, or an Asian metropolitan center. By the time they complete this book, or a coaching session or workshop with me, my clients know what their unique value is and what their irresistible offer is to the world.

What I've learned wasn't taught in college, but by being in the trenches with well-known figures. I have been fortunate to meet many amazing personalities including notable names like Oprah Winfrey, Whoopi Goldberg, Julia Roberts, Carol Burnett, Betty White, Hillary Clinton, Rita Moreno, and Robin Williams.

Whether it was a brief encounter, a sit-down interview, or a coaching session, every celebrity has taught me something about the *art of self-promotion* and communication.

They have all been phenomenal teachers—kind, deliberate, and inspiring. I have great respect for what they have shown me through the years. It is my first-hand experience and work with celebrities, media personalities, entertainment executives, and subject-matter experts that are the foundation of my overall coaching approach.

My passion and overall perspective on how we all have the potential to shine comes from two decades in and around the world of entertainment. I've adapted this experience to help individuals, professionals, and businesses use Hollywood skills to promote and brand themselves. My mission is to share what I've seen, experienced, and studied so that I may empower *you* with a blueprint to express your best self—to ***be an everyday celebrity and shine***.

Introduction

Put aside the props you use in presentations, the PowerPoint you create for board meetings, and the one-liners you use to meet someone at a bar. Can you depend on your own confidence and charisma to guide you instead?

Can you stand tall in a room full of strangers to speak your truth? Or give a presentation that will land you the deal of a lifetime? Or try to build up the courage to ask someone out and get to know her better?

It just takes commitment. You can bring out your own superstar quality, just by being your best self in everyday living. It begins with the decision to be deliberate and purposeful.

When celebrities are self-revealing and authentic, their stars really shine. The secret is: if you present your authentic self, you can shine like a celebrity, too—in your personal and professional life.

A simple yet powerful goal of this book is for you to discover your own *star quality*. That is the art of being authentic. It is the only way to set yourself apart from the competition.

My fundamental belief is that we are mediums, each of us, and *we have the ability to show others what we want them to see, experience, and believe about us.*

Success depends on communicating with intention,

purpose, and clarity.

Being authentic, though sometimes challenging, is the only way to truly set yourself apart. ***Everyday Celebrity*** aims to instill confidence in what people believe and say about themselves. It's time to unleash the authentic you waiting to be seen.

How to Use This Book

This book is intended to help you create your own blueprint for authentic self-promotion. In each chapter, I share stories from celebrities, high-profile personalities, executives, and other extraordinary people who might otherwise consider themselves ordinary. They are all people I've had the pleasure to interview or coach throughout my career.

Celebrities have shown me that authenticity can thrive in an unlikely industry, the entertainment business. They have built careers under the spotlight and are examples of how to cultivate an *irresistible offer*—a distinct and unique opportunity that comes from your truest and most extraordinary place of being, and promote it with a powerful, yet genuine, presence.

After each narrative and set of stories, there are key lessons learned from the exchange. Insights from the interactions might apply to your own quest for better self-promotion, greater presentation presence, and overall effective communication.

Give some thought to the stories. Then to help you create your own communication blueprint, there will be:

- a brief summary at the end of each chapter
- an exercise at the end of each chapter

- coaching tips for each of the 3Cs (confidence, clarity, charisma) at the end of their respective sections
- quick reference guides at the end of the book that include:
  - the 12 celebrity branding principles
  - key terms
  - celebrity branding flow chart

In the end, my goal is for you to realize that you have *celebrity essence*— the ability to select what to reveal about yourself, how to show it, and in what circumstances.

It begins with discovering your authentic self.

SECTION I:

The World of Celebrity

CHAPTER 1

Celebrity Self-Promotion

Celebrity Branding Principle: **The world of celebrity is fueled by self-promotion. Superstars show the world what they want others to see.**

We feel we "know" celebrities and public figures, but the undeniable truth is that we know very little about them—except for what they want us to know. We are familiar only with their public persona—one that they, by and large, control. Even their mishaps can be spun into positive publicity.

Celebrities are strategic, but they do not do it alone. The bigger the celebrity, the more extensive the Hollywood machine they have behind them. Agents, managers, publicists, producers, and studio or network executives help promote and protect their personality-driven brands. Many celebrities also employ wardrobe stylists, hair stylists, makeup artists, personal trainers, and even plastic surgeons and cosmetic dentists—an entire team to make them look and feel their best. On top of that, there may be advisors such as voice coaches, acting teachers, and mentors to help sharpen their skills.

The celebrity *brand* operates like a business. At the core of it is a personality: the celebrity.

Keeping the celebrity's brand on track is where I jump in. As a media coach, I work with the stakeholders—the team of publicity professionals and other advisors—to make sure that when celebrities, public figures, production executives, or media personalities open their mouths, they don't blow it.

Behind the scenes, I coach them on what to say and how to say it.

My philosophy is called *the art of authentic promotion* and the premise is simple: find something genuine and special in a star, promote it, and let it shine.

I'm a wordsmith advocate of purposeful and authentic messaging. I am a verbal brand engineer—one that not only deconstructs what truly makes that person special, but also helps him or her decide what to reveal and how to show it.

Knowing how to self-promote and create a positive public

image, something celebrities do on a daily basis, is a skill all of us can learn. You can sparkle like a celebrity, whether it's in your personal or professional life. Using self-promotion practices from the world of entertainment can help you embody the same kind of *powerful presence.*

This is the ability to communicate your best self. It can impact your relationships, careers, collaborations, and social lives.

Using Hollywood and U.S. media promotional tactics can help you professionally, such as performing better during a job interview, effectively promoting your business, and effortlessly navigating a press interview. But it doesn't stop there. Hollywood tactics can also help you personally, such as engaging at cocktail parties, going on successful dates, and resolving personal conflicts.

Whether you realize it or not, you practice self-promotion every day. From an early age you learned to automatically tailor your words and your stories based on your relationships and context. For example, as a child what you shared with your parents was distinctly different from what you shared with a friend. You have unknowingly been trained to deliberately reveal to others what you want them to know. This skill needs to be built upon.

You do not have to be somebody else, or what you believe others want you to be, in order to shine. Let's take a look at one of the most profound examples I've had the pleasure to witness.

The Queen of the Spotlight

I once produced what was probably the most amazing interview of my career. I was working for ABC television in San Francisco, California. It was a bright, sunny afternoon at Stanford University when I arrived with a six-person crew and a talk show host of Chinese descent.

We were all very excited and slightly anxious as we prepared for the Queen to arrive on set. Please know that I address her here in the most affectionate and admiring way possible. Interviewing one of the most prominent figures in U.S. media can be a daunting, yet exhilarating experience for a small group of production professionals. Engaging TV royalty was something we didn't take lightly. We were about to meet Ms. Oprah Winfrey.

When she arrived, Oprah Winfrey indeed embodied what it meant to be royalty. Dressed impeccably from head to toe, she wore a beautiful white summer dress and joked how it might flare up on camera, but smiled and said she knew we could take care of it. She was witty, kind, and personable. Over the next hour together, she shared her experience of being both a private individual and well-known popular figure. Everyone on the set was captivated. Afterward she took a photo with us, which I still treasure today.

Among the many wonderful things she said that afternoon, one especially powerful moment stands out. Toward the end of the interview my host turned to her and said, "Many people refer to me as the Asian Oprah. What advice do you have for me?"

Oprah's response was gracious, straightforward, and powerful. She thanked her for the compliment and said, in essence, that she shouldn't compare herself to her or anyone else.

When Oprah looked at her, she said she saw an incredibly likeable and beautiful woman. Oprah's following message was simple, yet profound: "Be the best person *you* can possibly be.

Go out there in the world, be yourself, and shine like no other."

Those words lingered in the air, and though I may have heard these same sentiments in similar ways from other people, when the Queen spoke them, they resonated. She, a masterfully successful force in the entertainment business, reminded us that to be powerful and make our mark in the world means to be authentic and true.

Whether this individual is an executive for Disney, a doctor on TV, performer, actor, or corporate professional, Oprah Winfrey's inspirational message encourages all to: "Go out there in the world, be yourself, and shine like no other."

The Showrunner

In contrast, years later I coached an executive producer, or "showrunner" as they are called frequently in TV, on his leadership and communication skills. The showrunner of a TV show is the head producer or creative lead who is primarily responsible for the day-to-day management of the production. Marc (not his real name) was a likeable guy—kind, considerate, and committed. Yet with all these great attributes, something was lacking. Concerned about how he was coming across, he was uneasy about his tone with network executives and his staff. He thought he did not come across as powerful enough. His essence seemed forced.

While I did not work directly with him or see him in action on set, from what he shared, combined with my previous TV experience, I did assess that he was thorough, and a capable leader.

Yet a nagging voice in his head kept him from truly being a star.

During one of our early sessions he asked me a question

that truly exemplified his thinking. "Can you give me a few examples of leaders who you feel have a commanding tone?" he asked. "I'd like to observe their body language and hear the words they use."

While his comments indicated a desire to be an effective leader, I felt he was really saying, "I want to act like someone else. I want to emulate the right communication style."

Marc was looking for *how* to be like somebody else. Even though looking at others as examples can be valuable, they should not be used as a comparison for what you should do or how you should act. He was ignoring *what* was appropriate for the given situation. *How* to act indicates that there is a certain way to be. *What* to act on gives you options and choices.

Each crisis, whether it was a delay in production or a 360-degree change that was suddenly mandated from the network, gave Marc an opportunity to examine "what" he valued at that moment. It gave him an opportunity to examine what kind of leader he wanted to be. This is quite different from *how* to act, which indicates that there is a set formula or solution that simply requires a set of predetermined steps—follow step one, then two, and so on.

A leader is most effective when he looks at the context of the situation. In other words, a leader looks at variables and values, not just *how* to react.

Over the course of a few sessions, Marc began shifting his perspective from doing the "right thing" or acting a certain way to truly evaluating what was needed in a given situation. This allowed him more freedom, both from being trapped in his head and from trying "to be" somebody or something.

We can change our perspective from thinking there is a right way "to be" to examining what we value in our heart that needs to be done. We sometimes may make the right decision and other times not. Either way, I believe we will be more successful, even in those moments we think we fail, by being who we are and not what we believe we should be.

Lesson Learned

There is no right or wrong way

The Queen and *The Showrunner* both showed me a lesson in personal character. Being genuine in your approach, open to possibilities, and sincere in your communication, helps bring out your own star power. There is no set formula for being effective and powerful in your career. True success lies within you. All you have to do is tap into it.

Oprah, in particular, shows us this in two very powerful points:

1. Appreciate the power of the spotlight. Whenever or however you are called to speak, understand that your words have meaning. You and your ideas are influential in ways that you may not know, and people will take away something from what you say—whether it is positive or discouraging. So, *make the moment count.* You are a medium. You convey a message, not only with your words, but with your entire being.

2. Do not fall into the trap of thinking that you have to be somebody else in order to shine like a star. In spite of being fired from a broadcast job early in her career, the experience prompted Oprah to find her voice and great success in another way, as a talk show host. So, too, can each of us find our path.

We can discover our true authentic voice and let it be heard. We—you, me and those we love—do not have to speak a certain way, do "the right thing" or follow a certain path set by others in order to be media royalty or superstars. All we have to do is be ourselves, act with gratitude in those moments when the spotlight shines on us, and illuminate as a star in our own world.

Summary

- Celebrities are strategic about self-promotion.
- Knowing how to self-promote and create a positive public image is a skill that all of us can learn and use in our lives.
- You don't have to be somebody else to be a star; you only have to be your best self.
- Find something genuine and special in you, promote it and let it shine. This is *the art of authentic promotion*.

Exercise

1. Take a sheet of paper and fold it in half.
2. Think about the times you compared yourself to someone you considered a success, such as a great leader or a superstar in a specific work or sports field. What qualities did that individual have that you admired? Write those in the right-hand column.
3. Next, consider the qualities you have that make *you* a superstar—the ways in which you shine. Write those on the left-hand side of the paper.
4. Compare the two lists and ask yourself:
   - Are the characteristics you admire in others those

qualities you wish you had or those that mirror the qualities you already have?

- Do you foster your personal strengths or try to be like someone else? Does that work? Why or why not?

The Call to Action

Identify when and how you fall into the trap of trying to be like somebody else.

CHAPTER 2

Who is a Celebrity?

Celebrity Branding Principle: **We are all celebrities. Yes, every single one of us.**

We all have the ability to stand out and be exceptional. Being a celebrity is to be seen and heard: to step into your own personal spotlight whether it is at work, at home, or in the community. It is to essentially show up and be noticed, and it starts with that first step on stage—both literally and metaphorically.

Hollywood is filled with celebrities, media personalities, and network executives who are under an intense microscope. One thing all actors, musicians, politicians, writers, TV hosts, and on-camera experts I've had the pleasure to work with have in common is they are constantly challenged to self-promote. Their success or failure depends significantly on popular opinion. They are called to show up on big platforms like TV talk shows and news reports, popular magazine interviews, social media, blogs, and in-person press conferences.

You, too, are a celebrity in your own area of life. And, while the scale is different, the core idea is the same: you are called to self-promote. You are the representative of your own personal brand.

In marketing the word "brand" refers to a product and the attributes it has that creates customer loyalty. What is personal branding? It is how you connect to your audience(s), sustain their trust, and remain accountable to them. It is the promise you make that distinguishes you and your irresistible offer.

How do personal brands show up? Let's take a look at two different celebrities from two very different worlds. They represent two very different brands. One is a TV star and the other is a stay-at-home mom.

The Heiress

In the advent of reality television, ordinary people were put into extraordinary situations. For example, they were asked to live in a house with strangers who had totally different backgrounds and lifestyles or forced to compete with skilled adversaries for food and shelter. We, as viewers, got to observe how these willing, ordinary everyday people handled the conflict and drama that arose from fabricated, yet lifelike scenarios. Pretty soon, stars were born from many of these programs, as formerly unknown individuals captured the spotlight.

Then celebrities got into the game.

That was good news for me because I was often hired to coach them: former child stars, relatives of current celebrities, heirs to fortunes, and even old time Hollywood actors as they prepared for press interviews.

They were used to being in the spotlight, but in this context—in a reality show where they were out of their element from their "normal" lives—was something new. They were called to be fishes out of water and were plopped into scenarios unfamiliar to them.

Here's an example of one such session. My colleagues and I arrived and walked into a large conference room at one of the administrative offices of a large studio lot. There sat a producer, publicists, and a set of empty chairs. We took our assigned seats and waited for the heiress to arrive. Moments later, the doors opened and in walked this impeccably dressed, well-made-up, larger-than-life celebrity with designer labels from head to toe, accentuated with expensive, trendy sunglasses. She took her seat across from us and one of the two production executives she walked in with introduced us. In charge of creating and promoting the series, these executives hired us to prepare her for upcoming print and broadcast interviews. They wanted her to perform well in the press because great answers and teasers about the program meant more viewers.

Now it was our turn. We started by describing the media coaching process, which included mock interviews, delineating talking points, identifying potential blind spots when answering questions, storytelling exercises, and reviewing best practices for clear, confident, and charismatic communication. We also declared our intention to help her express herself to the best of her ability, pull out captivating stories that would draw in the audience, and share her experience in a way that others would relate to and enjoy. To do so, we asked her to be open and fully engage the process.

Our purpose was to cultivate her voice, not make her into a cookie-cutter spokesperson for the network. Note: I still establish these same ground rules with all my coaching clients today. It is important that I am of service to them personally, as well as to the bigger picture, such as the show, project, or business.

As we described the process to the entire room that day, I couldn't help but feel somewhat intimidated because there were two chief executive officers (CEOs) of the production company who produced the show, a producer, and two publicists. They were all part of the machine behind this enterprise and were deeply invested in this celebrity and program.

From what we could tell, they listened to us intently because we could see their eyes as they nodded in acknowledgement. Meanwhile, the heiress sat sideways in her chair, giving us a profile of her face as she looked straight ahead toward the window, all while still wearing her stylish sunglasses.

After this exchange, it was time to get down to business. Our first course of action was to conduct a mock interview. We wanted to see her natural speaking style, rhythm, and personal charm. I was at bat. I moved closer to her. Sitting in typical interview position across from her, we were now face-to-face. She still had her sunglasses on, so I kindly asked, "Can you take off those sunglasses?"

No response.

I asked again, "I'd love to see those beautiful eyes of yours."

Again, I got nothing from her. I sat for a moment and thought, "How can I break through?" Determined, I tried a different strategy. I re-approached with humor, while trying not to be too snarky. "I need to see you without a barrier. You can't wear sunglasses in an interview."

She turned to the executive producers, the owners of the production company, as if asking for guidance. They nodded, and that was all it took to affirm my request. She took off the sunglasses and we started our mock interview. From that moment on, she was engaging and witty, often laughing at herself when she recounted her wacky adventures on the show.

She "showed up" in two remarkably different ways. At first, she established herself as the cool celebrity. Then, she let her guard down, just enough, and with the permission of the stakeholders in the room, engaged in a charming and personable fashion. She was keenly aware of her audience. In this example, her audience was "the media" with yours truly playing the role of a journalist.

A true celebrity, she has the skill set and experience to know when to amp it up and when to shift her energy to engage differently. She knows how she wants to present herself—to be friendly in certain situations and mysterious in others. As a personal brand she knows how to distinguish herself and connect with an audience.

The Farmer

In contrast, I met another lovely woman, the farmer, years later who didn't know she even had a choice on how to present herself. It was during my very first communication workshop in Taiwan, with Emily Liu, international leadership consultant and founder of *AsiaWorks* Taiwan, a prestigious professional and personal development training company.

The room was filled with people from all different kinds of backgrounds. Half the attendees were young Taiwanese celebrities who came to sharpen their promotional skills. The others were mainly professionals and CEOs who wanted to improve their professional and personal communication skills. There were also two people who had never been to any AsiaWorks training workshops. Mine was their first entry into personal development.

Of course, there are always students who speak up often. You may remember the type from grade school—and this workshop had many of them—the attention seekers who hog the spotlight. On the opposite end of the spectrum are those who rarely say anything. The farmer was one of them.

It was not until the second day that the group knew anything about the farmer. She was one of the two who had never been to a workshop like this. None of us had any idea what she did for a living. About an hour into that day's session, at a critical point in the workshop, she stood up and said, "I am not exceptional or great. I am just a mother and farmer. I have nothing of value to share or promote."

As she stood in the middle of the room making her assessments of worth, Emily gave me a look that said, "Take this and run with it."

I probed the farmer a little more about her assessments

and she continued with the same mantra, "I am not a professional. I don't have anything to contribute. I am just a farmer and a mom."

Then, I brought her to the front of the room and asked, "Why don't you think being a mom is valuable?"

She stopped, looked down, and said, "Because I am not important."

What happened next was phenomenal. I asked the room what they thought of her and almost all of the participants in the room rallied around her. They proclaimed to this farmer and mom what they had always wanted to say to their own moms. Some gave her praise while others asked for forgiveness. Their hearts, words and tears were filled with deep appreciation and admiration.

For the next few hours, she was the celebrity in the room. All eyes were on her. She was in the spotlight. She was the one everyone wanted to know.

The farmer shined, and the entire time she remained genuine, open, and sincere. As the day progressed, she went from being "just a mother and farmer" to standing tall, with certainty and confidence.

There Is a Choice

The choice to be or not to be stellar becomes known the moment we step forward and are seen. It is that moment when eyes and ears are focused on us. It doesn't matter whether we choose the spotlight or not. What we do in that spotlight is a decision we make beforehand. We can be prepared or not. We can be aware of our value or we can choose to ignore it.

We can be like the heiress and in charge of our identity, or we can be like the farmer, completely convinced that we are not exceptional at all. The heiress played up her grandeur. She chose when and how to show certain parts of her personality. The farmer, on the other hand, was oblivious to her power.

While that may be fine for some, I suspect you wouldn't even be reading this book if that's what you wanted for yourself.

Lesson Learned

You are exceptional

The point of this story is to acknowledge that you are exceptional. Next, make a commitment to show it. At this point, don't be concerned about how and in what ways. Just own it. Then others will respond to the authentic you that shines through. Marianne Williamson puts this nicely in her book, *A Return to Love* (Harper One, 1996):

"As we let our own light shine, we unconsciously give other people permission to do the same. As we are liberated from our own fear, our presence automatically liberates others."

Summary

- We all have the ability to stand out and be exceptional in our own area of expertise or life. It's a choice.
- You are the representative of your own personal brand.
- Acknowledge that you are exceptional. Make a commitment to show it.
- You choose to how to shine in the spotlight.

Exercise

1. Write down in what ways and in what circumstances you are like the heiress. Do you show up authentically or put on a show? How does this serve you?
2. Write down in what ways and in what circumstances you are like the farmer. How does this serve you?

The Call to Action

Ask yourself: what is one authentic shift I can make today to shine brighter at work, at home, or with friends?

SECTION II:

Celebrity Essence

CHAPTER 3

What Is Celebrity Essence?

Celebrity Branding Principle: **Being a star is not a state of mind; it's a way of being.**

We show others how to treat us. We tell others what to think of us. The farmer in the previous story had no idea what she was communicating about herself. Because she felt she had no value, she chose to be invisible. This was an unconscious decision, but still, it was a decision. She never knew until her spotlight moment that being exceptional was even an option. We, too, can choose to be seen or not be seen. We choose whether or not to reveal our exceptional selves.

The heiress, on the other hand, knew she was exceptional. She also understood that she could tailor what was shown to others. She had the power to be seen the way she wanted to be seen.

Selecting what to reveal, how to show it, and in what circumstances, is what celebrities do regularly. Like the heiress, we can choose what part of ourselves we want to share and promote publicly.

This awareness is the foundation of what I call *celebrity essence.*

Celebrity essence is letting personal *star quality* shine: standing tall, with your feet planted firmly in the ground and knowing with certainty that you are a gift to the world. *Celebrity essence* is selecting what personal strengths and attributes you want to show others. *Celebrity essence* is the sincere conviction to be purposeful and strategic with your public identity.

Celebrity essence is not rooted in vanity. You simply know your potential, take control of it, and foster your *star quality.*

Too many times we surrender our power. There are a myriad of reasons, such as our upbringing, why we choose to step into the background and abdicate responsibility over our own identity. A psychologist could explain these reasons in great detail. For our purposes I will share my firsthand experience on how public figures, both the veterans and newbies, choose or relinquish authority over their stardom.

To help illustrate this point a little further, let's look at *Old Hollywood* and *New Hollywood.*

Old Hollywood

Early in my career, I worked for an entertainment-based cable network producing celebrity biographies. The great thing about this TV program was that all the stars were still living and I met some amazing well-known personalities, as well as their families, friends, and colleagues. The purpose of this particular series was to inspire and entertain viewers with stories about a celebrity's upbringing, accomplishments, and any adversities he or she overcame on the road to success. I enjoyed witnessing these stars on a level not often seen by others. I had the opportunity to delve into their childhoods, trials and tribulations, and everything that made them the people we love and admire.

I had the pleasure of interviewing well-known comedians, highly respected figures in the entertainment business, and award-winning actors. Many began their careers doing stand-up, performing on Broadway, or working odd jobs in Los Angeles until they were "discovered." Some had the classic Hollywood success story, while others endured roadblock after roadblock on their journeys to stardom. All of them, however, dealt with real life circumstances just like all of us. One of my favorites was a sharp-witted, comedic actor who charmed audiences on and off screen.

He was gracious with his time and let us in to his private bubble. In addition to sitting down with him, my team interviewed his family, friends, and other key figures in his life. We asked questions about his youth and explored experiences that helped shape this talented performer. One of the most heart-wrenching stories we discussed was the unexpected passing of his father. He was a teenager when his father died of a stroke. This dramatic event impacted the entire family and as everyone recounted the story, they became very emotional. When his mom shared her point of view, she broke down in tears.

Once we edited the interviews and assembled the entire episode, we reviewed the show. One of the network executives was concerned about the sequence in which we showed his family members crying over the death of his father, because she felt it was too sensational. She believed an emotional outpouring was unnecessary for an already emotional story. After some discussion, my team was asked to re-edit that portion and deleted the moment his mother got teary-eyed as a simple way of respecting their privacy.

Even with the compromise, the story remained strong without it.

But why did the network executive care? Why did we care? More importantly would the actor care?

We did it in consideration of an unspoken boundary. Simply put, the way his mother was portrayed in reaction to his father's death was personal to the actor. We respected that because he had nothing to hide. He gave us full access to all the people in his life, including his family. He would not deny the impact of his father's passing, but how it was revealed would make a difference to him. There was no need to add unnecessary drama to an already emotional situation.

He knew the value of his personal brand and the power behind it. He, like many in what I call "Old Hollywood" (those performers with experience and wisdom in self-promotion), is in control of his image. He knows how he wants to come across and how detailed to be with his personal life. He has integrity and does not compromise it.

In contrast, some celebrities are thrown into the spotlight, either unexpectedly or on purpose, who feel they need to do everything possible to remain in it, even to the point of selling out. This weakens their brand. Others are just not prepared and haven't thought it through. They feel their light needs to shine at maximum illumination or not at all. The pitfall is that they can easily burn out. They either put too much fuel into the flame or not enough. In either case, they acquiesce to the attention and surrender their ability to navigate and truly benefit from the spotlight.

I am sure you can think of a few celebrities right now who fit this mold. If not, tune into the news tonight and you are sure to see one.

Young Hollywood

Hollywood lives in many places—from the soundstages in Vancouver, Canada, and location shoots in New Zealand to the music studios in London and the dramatic theaters of Beijing. Hollywood is not confined to a geographic location. It is the entertainment business at large. It is where celebrities and performers are called to speak into the microphone, perform for an online audience or stand, front and center, on stage.

For the rest of us there is a metaphorical Hollywood in our lives. It exists in situations and places where we are called to stand out and shine, such as board meetings or networking events.

At an AsiaWorks communication workshop, my co-facilitator, Emily Liu, and I discovered our own Hollywood in Taipei. At the beginning of the first day, we asked participants to introduce themselves. A few of them showed up in a big way. Two of the participants got up and sang immediately. And they were not amateurs. They were outstanding. A few others offered a touch of theatrics and drama throughout the workshop.

I remember four of them in particular. I like to refer to them as the performer, the model, the sex symbol, and the international singer. They were "Young Hollywood" at its best.

These four members of Young Hollywood knew the value of good self-promotion. They used every medium available to promote themselves, from social media to conventional press. In fact, Jimmy, whom I call the international singer, had gained worldwide popularity online and was invited to the "real" Hollywood to appear on the Ellen DeGeneres Show. He and the others knew their exceptional talents and did not shy away from showing them.

I admired how certain and determined they were to shine. I wish I'd had that sort of fortitude in my early twenties. They were spirited, self-assured, and determined to be stars.

As the weekend unfolded, something else became apparent about them. They did not know when to share the spotlight. They were always "on." While they were aware of themselves individually, they lacked the experience of knowing when to dial up the attention-seeking and when to dial it down.

Sometimes the best way to improve public identity is to be *gracious*. This means giving the spotlight to others. There is context to consider: look at the time and place—and the situation you find yourself in.

There are moments when you can make more of an

impression by choosing not to be the center of attention. In these instances, take a chance, even if that means being more self-revealing. Seize an opportunity to connect on a personal level and not make it all about you when you speak.

For example, maybe you can tell a story about a positive influence that helped shape your life, a story about someone that helped you overcome a struggle, or a break-up that inspired you to be a better person.

Connection is something all of us seek and desire. We want to relate to others and share common experiences. Look at the actors from Old Hollywood that you feel you "know."

The same is true for all of us. Think about a networking event when you meet someone for the first time. You don't want to just know his or her job title; you want to know a little bit about the person behind the position. You want to connect with another human being—a perfectly imperfect person.

So often our desire to project perfection keeps us from revealing any sort of vulnerability. However, it's not an all-or-nothing proposition. It's about creating boundaries where you know you are safe to dance and play. It is also about finding moments to create what I like to call *alignment opportunities*, those instances in which you find common ground, shared experiences, and similar interests with others.

Alignment opportunities could be finding out you enjoy the same movies, endured similar financial struggles, or have complementary personality traits.

Alignment opportunities are a key element to building relationships. They require you to share a little something about yourself. Ideally what you share is based on a commonality that you've noticed in the other individual or group.

Alignment opportunities also require trust. You are called to take a chance by revealing something intimate about you or your background. What you choose to share and how you share it is up to you. Quite often, determining the boundaries of personal self-revelation is a trial-and-error process, but it is one many of us have been working on for most of our lives.

At the workshop in Taiwan, the Young Hollywood stars were challenged to find *alignment opportunities*. They had to be vulnerable—just enough to make a connection. This is true for all of us, whether it is in business or our own personal Hollywood.

The performer, the model, the sex symbol, and the international singer had to learn to share and pull others into the spotlight. In doing so, they didn't shine any less. In fact, they discovered that they shined brighter because they connected to the audience in an *authentic* and sincere way. They no longer were just performing for them; they were a part of them.

They had a special gift: being able to draw other people out of their shells. They were all innately gracious and loving people who wanted to share a part of themselves to make others happy. This will help them profoundly as their careers grow.

Lesson Learned

You are in control

Each of us is in control of our public image. We choose what can and should be revealed about ourselves, even when we decide to surrender our power. We dim or brighten our light. Just like Old Hollywood, we can create boundaries around our public story. And like Young Hollywood, we can learn when to be gracious for the sake of building trust and relationships. Knowing in advance what to do when you are the center of attention is essential.

Your *celebrity essence*, or ability to self-promote, requires planning and a personal blueprint.

What areas of your life or background are you willing to reveal and what areas do you choose to keep private? Keep in mind, what you share may change through time. For example, celebrities who were in the closet for years have since come out as gay. Others who have dealt with substance abuse and hid it have later shared their struggles and triumphs.

For years, I had buried the experience of being bullied as a child, taunted because of my lisp. It was humiliating. I carried that shame for a long time. However, as I began speaking more, my desire to truly connect with my audience grew.

As I started to more deeply share my personal experience along with my professional learning, my work blossomed. I had put into practice the courage I coach others to seek in their own communication. This story made me vulnerable, but it was in those moments when I let my guard down that I knew people understood my pain—and determination to overcome the humiliation.

We are all vulnerable, but taking that leap of faith can reap rewards for both sides. My vulnerability made me stronger because I shared it. Audiences began relating to me not only as a coach, but also as a person who struggled with his own self-confidence and ability to communicate.

The same can happen for you if you are daring enough to embrace your potential weakness or setback as an opportunity to grow and become stronger. Your story can inspire others. The power of empathy allows us to see greatness in others and ourselves. When we let down those walls, we connect on a very different, very real, very authentic level.

Summary

- We show others how to treat us. We tell others what to think of us.
- *Celebrity essence* is based in knowing with certainty how you want others to see and experience you.
- Being a celebrity does not require being "on" all the time.
- Share the spotlight.
- Find *alignment opportunities* to connect with others.

Exercise

1. Identify five key stories in your life that you feel helped shape you as a person.
2. Pinpoint the lesson learned in each and the relatable

elements in it that might endear you to others.

3. Break down the essential points of each story into three to five bullet points.

4. On a scale of one to five, score each story with the ease in which you are willing to share it, with one being the least comfortable and five being the most comfortable.

5. Afterward, choose the top three stories.

6. Share one of the stories with a friend and gauge the feedback. Did the listener respond favorably? Did you feel more connected? Was the message effectively received?

The Call to Action

Get comfortable with the idea of being self-revealing and realize that you already have the skills to tell your own story quite well. It may feel scary at first, but choose what you will share, how you will share it, and when you will share it.

This call to action is an act of courage.

CHAPTER 4

The 3C's of Celebrity Essence

Celebrity Branding Principle: **Celebrity essence is the embodiment of a unique powerful presence.**

I am often asked, "How do you nurture your *celebrity essence*?" At its core, *celebrity essence* requires three traits: (1) Clarity, (2) Confidence, and (3) Charisma. These are the 3Cs.

Celebrities constantly sculpt their image via intentional self-promotion. They choose what to reveal about their lives. Those who are successful in managing their public identity utilize the 3Cs:

1. They have *clarity* in what they want to communicate.
2. They show up with *confidence* because they believe in who they are and the value they have to others.
3. They have *charisma*—a personal style of connecting with others based on their authentic being.

What does this mean for you?

It doesn't matter if you're in Hollywood, if you're on TV, if you're a musician selling a record, or an actor promoting a movie—each of us has moments when we are called to be center stage. Tapping into your *celebrity essence* is to know your personal power. Knowing your power allows you to be more effective in your life. It helps you set your goals, reach them, and build confidence in yourself—to know that you can do it—whatever it is that you want to accomplish.

It is important for you to identify and manage the message you give to others about yourself. Whether it is starting a business, looking for a new job, or maintaining influence—the way that you come across and the public identity you present will significantly impact the results.

Are you clear, confident, and charismatic in your approach? Do you utilize the 3Cs?

By exploring each one of the 3Cs, you cannot only improve your *celebrity essence*—you can also measure it. We call this measurement your *Celebrity Quotient* *(CQ)*. You can specifically identify the overall impression you want to make on others.

Think of it this way: when you walk away from a meeting, what do you want people to remember? For example, do you want them to say, "She is trustworthy, smart, and confident"? Or do you want them to think, "That was an interesting presentation."

We have a tremendous amount of leverage and influence on how people perceive and experience us. They witness what we show them. The 3Cs help sculpt what we reveal.

Let's delve further into this by analyzing how *The Comedian* brings the 3Cs to life.

The Comedian

I loved watching comedies as a child. I spent hours in front of the TV laughing at the crazy antics of other characters that usually resulted from a misunderstanding, mishap, or miscalculation of one sort or another. My early childhood friend who watched many of these shows with me was my Grandma Grace—the same woman who early on told me I would grow up one day to entertain people.

The two of us spent hours side-by-side, watching one of her favorite TV shows, *I Love Lucy*. She was a fan of the show, not only because of the redhead's wacky shenanigans, but also because she considered Lucille Ball a role model of someone who made the most of life and celebrated it. I believe Grandma Grace's influence early in my TV viewing days gave me a deep appreciation for female comedians and also impacted the way I viewed the world.

In comedies there always seems to be some sort of confusion or unexpected event that creates havoc out of an everyday situation. This is true of life, as well. What make these circumstances manageable are the right attitude and the right approach. Part of comic relief (and "relief" is the key word) is the ability to laugh at oneself and not approach life too rigidly.

At the same time, characters in comedy shows are resourceful when facing unusual circumstances. This employs two characteristics: (1) being self-aware and (2) choosing to be present in a situation.

When you can smile and take life on life's terms, you can move forward. Comedy shows resilience and that you can be grounded in grace and appreciation.

Celebrities like Ellen DeGeneres and Sandra Bullock exemplify this kind of attitude. The comedic roles they choose are resilient and flexible, while maintaining a degree of integrity.

Though I've not had the pleasure to meet these two talented stars, in 2002, I interviewed and spent the morning with Carol Burnett and the cast of *The Carol Burnett Show* for a magazine photo shoot. It was thrilling to sit there and interview Ms. Burnett, Tim Conway, Harvey Korman and Vicki Lawrence. They are icons who helped change the face of TV forever.

I remember having to call Harvey Korman's "people" to confirm the interview. The person on the other end of the phone was his wife. The contact number I was given was actually his home number. Normally a star has people who help manage schedules and appearances. Harvey was an exception. He took charge of his own public relations and media strategy… and was good at it. He was down to earth and I had a lovely first interaction with him.

I also remember when it was time to interview Carol Burnett. She had just finished modeling for photos and came to sit down for our interview. After we started the interview, she paused and said, "Wait, I'm hungry. I'm going to get something to eat. Do you want anything?"

When I told her no, she insisted. "You've been here all morning so you must be hungry." Here she was, one of the queens of comedy, concerned about me. It was quite lovely and genuine.

Looking back on that day, I feel like I touched TV greatness. What made it so special was these stars' friendly, down-to-earth and grateful demeanor. As I spoke to Carol and her cast, they shared how much they loved the experience of acting on the *Carol Burnett Show*. The graciousness and gratitude practiced by these veteran celebrities warmed my heart. They knew how to shine.

It also makes me smile when I think about what made this show and cast stand out. I believe it comes down to a few magical lessons every one of us can learn from: (1) don't be afraid to laugh at yourself, (2) roll with your mistakes, and (3) stay connected with your surroundings and purpose.

If you have ever seen the *Carol Burnett Show*, then you know exactly what I am talking about. Each of these skills is important when we are called to step into our own personal spotlight.

Carol Burnett employed the 3Cs. She had *clarity*: her role was to entertain. She did this through a comedic look at life and events. She was *confident*: she knew that creating laughter was her gift and that it could help others smile, relax, and get away from the stressors of life. She had *charisma*: her natural skills to be endearing, witty, and likeable shined through in all of her scenes.

Whether it's doing a presentation or speaking in front of a group, I often think, "What would Carol Burnett do?"

I am not advocating being funny for the sake of being funny, but you must have the ability to not take yourself too seriously. Relax. You really can't make a mistake. Staying connected to your audience is essential to delivering something noteworthy. It is part of having *celebrity essence.*

The Everyday Celebrity

Celebrities like you and me, who are not actors, politicians, or professional athletes, often show up in a remarkable, yet subtle, fashion. Our celebrity essence can be strong, even though we are not performers in a Hollywood movie. We are the "everyday celebrity."

We have influence and impact on the world around us, even if we're not seen on the big screen. Some of us are reserved and quiet, while others are loud and bold. We are friends, role models, co-workers, loved ones, community leaders, and even strangers. We draw people into our *star quality* and, at times, may be a superstar to someone, though we don't always know it. Our impact is felt deeply and our influence, extraordinary.

For me, the first "everyday celebrity" I experienced in this way was my Grandma Grace. An emigrant from Mexico, she came to the United States as a young teenager. She traveled throughout the U.S. with her family as her father worked as a laborer helping to build the Santa Fe Railroad. Growing up I often heard her tell delightful stories of the prairielands in the Midwest and what life was like "back then."

Grandma Grace was a spectacular storyteller. Her family settled in a suburb roughly twenty miles outside of downtown Los Angeles, in a town known as Azusa. There she met a young, debonair man, whom she would eventually marry, my Grandpa Ray. Together, they had twelve children, forty-two grandchildren, and countless great-grandchildren. And while they had their own big family in this small community, they were also "grandparents" and role models, or at least it seemed, to all the citizens of Azusa.

Born of simple means, Grandma Grace treasured every adventure and challenge that came her way. While she didn't have a lot of monetary wealth, she always said she was rich in love and personal conviction. She struggled like all of us do on this journey of life—with children who passed away, illnesses, and financial woes—but always chose to let her personal, internal, and undeniable light shine. She provided for her children, went to church, worked in her garden, attended sporting activities, became an active member in her community, and always had time to listen to friends or family members in need.

I am reminded of the farmer who spoke out during that first workshop who felt she wasn't extraordinary. She was an everyday celebrity, just like my grandmother. The difference is that Grandma Grace knew what distinguished her from the farmer. Life wasn't about her; it was about her gift and service to others. She gave what she could because she knew the act of giving mattered.

She was my first personal superstar, and also a big reason why I am writing today, sharing my experiences, strength, and hope. While I could write pages and pages about her life and why she was so important to me, for our purposes, I want to share two facts.

First, the everyday superstar—you, me, each of us—has a tremendous influence on other people's lives. We are a gift to the world. Second, life is too short to worry about what you don't have. Live in the moment and celebrate the abundance around you.

She was one of my first friends and biggest fans. She encouraged me always to be my best authentic self. I never once felt she expected me to be anything different from who I was meant to be, a star in everything I did. That set me up for the life I lead today.

My grandmother's *celebrity essence* was not founded in pride. It was bold in other ways: she cared enough to give everything she could. Grandma Grace had the 3Cs. She had *clarity*: she knew she was a gift to others. People looked up to her. She was *confident*: she didn't worry so much about money. She was rich in other ways. Her value was being able to lend an ear, cook a tasty meal, offer advice, and simply put a smile on a young boy's face. She had *charisma*: her peaceful, loving spirit drew people to her. They wanted to be around her.

The comedian and the everyday celebrity are both icons— Carol in the world of comedy, and Grandma Grace in the world around her. I believe we can shine anywhere, anytime. Our metaphorical Hollywood is often right in front of us.

Lesson Learned

You can shine anytime, anywhere

Celebrity essence is built on the idea that you remain true to yourself. Showing up in the world, regardless of the context, is not trapped by ideas of how you "have to be" or "should be." For some of us that may be through humor, for others (like poets or dramatic writers) it may be deep sincerity, and for some (like journalists) it may be curiosity. Whatever the case, tapping into your own *celebrity essence* first requires being clear about the roles you play and how you show up in them.

Summary

- The 3Cs of *celebrity essence* are: Clarity, Confidence, and Charisma.
- You have control of the overall impression you want to make on others.
- Challenge your notions of how you "should" show up or how you "have to be."

Exercise

1. Think about key turning points in your life and the roles that developed from them. For example were there

significant moments when you felt compelled to be the "funny one" or the jester who eased tension? Were there moments where you had to be strong or the "soldier" who pushed forward?

2. What stories have you created about your character as a result of those turning points? Are you strong? Weak? Burdened? Determined?

3. Did the role you take on truly satisfy you?

The Call to Action

Reexamine the roles you've taken on at key turning points in your life. Explore how they've brought out the "real" you and how they might have also created a way you "have to be."

SECTION III:

Clarity

CHAPTER 5

What's Your Story?

Celebrity Branding Principle: **Shift your internal dialogue and witness yourself with clarity.**

We have a lot of dialogue circulating in our heads. Different voices shape the story we create about ourselves. This internal dialogue is often based on the narratives we've heard about "who we are" throughout our lives.

For example, my grandmother told me I made her laugh and smile. When she was laid up with a broken leg, the skits I performed for her lifted her spirits. She taught me that I was entertaining. I grew up believing it.

For others, similar stories from childhood, such as what it means to be a man or how to succeed, have helped shape the person they have become. As we continue on our journey of life, we carry these ideas and notions of "who we are" with us. The voices we've heard can be empowering or limiting. Sometimes a particular voice is so loud that we don't hear anything else.

When we share our own story—or speak about ourselves to others—we are interpreting who we are to the world. We are sharing the stories we've constructed about ourselves through the years. When people hear our words, thoughts and ideas, they interpret them further. For example, you may share with people that you have a master's degree in engineering. They hear—or interpret—"She is smart."

Often people do not remember the details of a story you convey, but they will remember the essence of it. You leave an impression.

Who are the masters of making impressions? Celebrities. Quite often when we see actors, performers, and other well-known people, we envision extraordinary individuals. We don't even know them, yet, in our minds, they are stars that shine in some remarkable way. Even when they are under a negative spotlight, we still focus on them.

Celebrities have our attention. They are constantly making

impressions on us. Some of us aspire to be well-known people, just like our favorite actors or performers. Others may want particular elements of stardom. It's natural and quite human, but in order for us to illuminate on any level, it is essential to mitigate the negative voices that consume our belief systems.

The tools in this chapter aim to help you get a sense of the celebrity that you have inside. If you don't feel like a star, you won't shine like one. More importantly, if you don't feel like a star, you choose to sell yourself short.

We have the ability to reveal certain parts of ourselves. We can shift and navigate what others see in us. It is an inside-out approach. Working on the outside alone, the physical manifestation of how you speak and present yourself will only help you so much. You must go inside to see how you show up for *yourself*. Then you can look at what you present to others.

We all have a public identity. The question is: how well does it represent your true exceptional being? Does the way others perceive you match the way you want to come across? To master the messages you give to others about yourself—the way you self-promote—requires looking at your internal dialogue and story, as well as examining the roles you play.

It Starts at an Early Age

Each of us controls our public identity. We convey messages about who we are to the world every day. We tell others how to treat us. As we touched upon in an earlier chapter, we learned how to do it at a very early age. As kids on the playground, we grasped almost immediately how to communicate with others. As kids, we identified that we have different relationships, and with these different relationships we play distinct roles.

For example, we learned to be a friend, a student or a son. The way we interacted in a given role and communicated was based on our relationship with the other person. We knew that the way we spoke to a parent was quite different from the words we used when speaking to a friend.

We carry this fundamental idea of relationships and roles with us into adulthood. For example, the way that I act with my friend, Eleanor, is very different from the way I interact with my mom, Patricia. There are stories, experiences, and language that I use with Eleanor that I don't feel comfortable using with my mom. That is not to say that I'm not truly *authentic*, or less sincere, in front of my mom. I'm just very clear about what I share with her. I do this because of my relationship with her. I don't want her to worry or meddle too much.

The point is that I choose, just like you, what to share and with whom. Is it sinking in?

The roles we play with others from childhood through adulthood help shape the way we communicate with others. We already know how to manage and control messages. This understanding is the foundation of having clarity, the first of the 3Cs.

Skid Row, Los Angeles

In addition to celebrities and entertainment executives, I have had the pleasure to coach and develop some pretty cool personality-driven brands and thought-leaders, from medical professionals, scientists, designers, and writers, to keynote speakers, amazing experts, and media personalities. One deeply rewarding experience I had was being the presentation coach for a few TEDx events, independently organized events in various communities that carry the mission of TED, which is "ideas worth sharing."

My first event was TEDx Skid Row. A former producer and current friend, Eyvette, who I met while working on a talk show together, gave up a successful career in entertainment to start a non-profit charity. When she started, she worked primarily through The Mission in Skid Row, Los Angeles. Skid Row is an urban, impoverished area with homeless and neglected people, and most live on the street. Her charity, Urban Possibilities, aims to help homeless men and women transition off the streets of Los Angeles by redefining their stories of self-doubt, neglect, addiction, and abuse. It's an amazing transformational organization that mirrors my own belief: that our internal dialogue shapes the story we reveal about ourselves to others.

Eyvette called me one afternoon and asked if I would media coach four young men. Two were still living in a homeless shelter. The other two had successfully made it out on their own, after having lived in the shelter. My job was to help them share their story in the context of a TEDx talk.

At first I thought, "How am I going to do this? I have nothing in common with them."

I discovered I had more in common with these four men than I could have imagined. They were smart, successful, and creative souls whose lives were traumatized by dramatic circumstances. Their stories were intense and powerful, yet, at the core, they did not truly comprehend their own value or personal strength.

They believed the roles and labels others had assigned to them: victim, abuser, drunk, criminal, degenerate, or loser. Others told them how they should act and, ultimately, how they should see themselves and feel about themselves.

They, with good reason, did not believe they could get

beyond those roles and labels.

Eyvette worked with them over the course of months to help redefine their individual stories of failure into stories of success. Her mission was, and is, to mine untapped human potential and turn despair into hope. My job was to help them step into the spotlight as speakers and leaders. I was there to coach them to proclaim a different story. I was there to encourage them to talk about their other roles, ones they had long forgotten, such as artist, executive, writer, father, healer, and brother.

Over the course of a few sessions, I worked with these men on their presentations. At first, like all of us, they were nervous. They were unclear on what to say. They had learned to bury their experiences in shame, doubt, and fear.

As they opened up, these fabulous speakers humbled me. Each of their personal stories had similar themes: strength, courage, and integrity, because that's what it takes to turn your life around on Skid Row.

How each of them got to Skid Row wasn't as important as how they changed their lives. As each of them hit their personal all-time low, when they didn't see any possibility of hope, and when none of us would see any possibilities regardless of our backgrounds, these men created change.

They had a powerful message: you can change. You can be your best self.

While the details of their personal stories and how they chose to express them were different, the common theme throughout was that of *hope*. This hope evolved organically from each of their real life experiences. They saw and were living a life of new possibilities.

Working on TEDx Skid Row was important to me on many levels. One of the most significant reasons is because it reinforced my belief about the power of stories. We are all storytellers, and the first story we learned to tell was our own.

The first conversation you have every day is with an audience of one: yourself. Choose your words wisely. Internal dialogue is powerful.

When we understand the innate power of our authentic story, we better connect to our audience, lover, family, clients, coworkers, and friends.

There is freedom to be just as you are. You can truly share the best part of you because you've already examined the worst part of you. And, guess what? You are okay with it. You don't have to pretend and worry about being found out.

Defining Roles

How can we fine-tune or even change our own stories? The first step is to get clear on our roles. Clarity, the first of the 3Cs, begins with an evaluation of the different ways we show up. How we naturally interact and present ourselves to others allows us to see the natural ways in which we speak, as well as how we show up publicly and personally, just as we did as children.

Let's look at two celebrity examples that we feel we may know. They have shown us, via press interviews, different aspects of their lives. They have masterfully revealed what they want us to know.

- Celebrity: Oprah
  Her Roles: TV Host, Actress, Philanthropist, Media Mogul

- Celebrity: Jeremy Lin
  His Roles: Professional Athlete, Son, Role Model, Christian

We, too, have the ability to reveal certain parts of ourselves. We can shift and navigate what others see in us. From the moment we begin interacting with others, we discover how to reveal certain parts of ourselves over another. We choose what to divulge and share with those around us. For example, I am a coach, friend, son, entrepreneur, and now, author.

AUTHOR   FRIEND

SON   COACH

Lesson Learned

Yours is a never-ending story

Why, then, are so many of us scared, anxious, or nervous about meeting someone new or speaking in front of co-workers? When the spotlight is on us, why do we hold ourselves back? If we can control the message, then why aren't we sharing it? We cannot fixate on a single story, one voice, or one role. The challenge is to break down the options available to us and reclaim the role and stories that best serve us.

Summary

- Different voices shape the story we create about ourselves.
- We learn at a very early age how to convey who we are to others.
- Understanding your different roles is the first step in gaining clarity on your individual *celebrity essence.*

Exercise

1. Take ten minutes to look at the different labels and roles of your personality and break them down.

2. Draw a diagram, split into four quadrants, similar to the one used in my example.

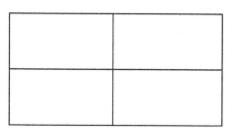

3. Insert the different roles into each of the quadrants. Write some characteristics of each role.
4. What parts of each role serve you? Which do not?

The Call to Action

Examine the ways in which your roles and labels have defined you. What's true? What's missing?

CHAPTER 6

The A Factor

Celebrity Branding Principle: **The key to unlocking powerful self-promotion lies within your ability to navigate between the audience, your agenda, and a call to action. This is The A Factor.**

Understanding how our roles, labels, and internal dialogue define us is the first step in creating clarity. The second step in creating clarity as it relates to communication is through a process I've developed called *The A Factor*.

The A Factor is the key to *the art of authentic promotion*.

It is one of the cornerstones for my work with all clients: celebrities, subject-matter experts, spokespeople, authors, media personalities, executives, and others—civilians and professionals alike—seeking to tap into their *star quality*.

The *art of authentic promotion* is a skill of communicating something extraordinary about you and your *irresistible offer* that is tailored to those who need to hear your message. It is a way of directly positioning yourself with clarity to a specific audience. It helps you get to the point more quickly and efficiently. With celebrities, this is used for press interviews to help develop good sound bites, which are quick, direct answers to interview questions.

Let's first look at the seductive term, *irresistible offer.* I initially heard this phrase from a coach at Newfield Network when he was trying to get me to enroll in the coaching certification program. Since then I've heard it used by others, and it stuck with me through the years.

The way I define *irresistible offer* is: a distinct and unique opportunity that comes from your truest self. When we tap into something truly authentic in ourselves, we are irresistible. If we present this part of ourselves to others we have an *irresistible offer.*

With those terms in mind, *The A Factor,* the *art of authentic promotion,* is broken into three key actions: know your audience, define an agenda, and create a call to action.

SPECIFIC AUDIENCE

+

DEFINED AGENDA

+

A DETAILED CALL TO ACTION

=

AUTHENTIC PROMOTION

While identifying audiences and tailoring messages to them may be a fundamental marketing concept, it's an important idea to keep in mind when it comes to self-promotion because often we may not think of ourselves as a product or personality brand. Celebrities do, and they do so masterfully. They know that their success depends on how an audience responds to their project, film, TV show, or social media post—and to them. They are at the center of their own business. How well they are received and respected as people determines their success.

In our transparent world—both with traditional media and social media—sculpting an image or business product is important because you must remain in the public's eye and keep yourself interesting. People not only want to know about their favorite personalities, it's expected. To that end, if all of us, not just celebrities, do not control the message that's out there about who and what we are, we leave it open to interpretation and manipulation.

For you, what does that mean? Audiences will make assumptions and assessments based on what they see and guess about you. There is no way to avoid having a public identity unless you hide from human interaction altogether.

Take charge of it: be strategic.

Let's delve a little deeper into the elements of *The A Factor*.

1. Audience: *Determine what matters most to those who need to hear what you have to say.*

When celebrities speak to a reporter, host, or journalist during a press interview, they are speaking not only to that individual, but also to his or her audience. The host/journalist represents a larger group who share a common background or interest. For example, the audience of a popular U.S. morning talk show is stay-at-home moms; meanwhile, the audience of an entertainment industry-related magazine is entertainment professionals.

When a celebrity speaks to the respective media outlet, he or she is speaking to a specific audience and, therefore, will tell different stories or pieces of information that are relevant to that demographic. The stay-at-home moms may be more interested in the camaraderie on set, with funny, behind-the-scenes antics, what that celebrity enjoys doing on the weekends, or how much he or she is like the character portrayed in the movie or TV show.

The entertainment industry-insiders may be more interested in filming techniques, the financial obligations to market the project, profit sharing, and the production timeline. Each of these audiences has different values and interests.

We also deal with different audiences in our everyday lives that have distinct values and interests. If you are going to be effective in your communication with them, then address what's important to them – not to you. What message do you have that they want to hear? Does he or she value financial success, education, fairness, a better quality of life, or something else? Every audience, whether it is an audience of one or an audience of 1,000, listens for something different. Respect their time and attention by giving them an answer, a solution, a challenge, an offer, or an opportunity that is of value *to them*.

For example, a business colleague may want to know the process and progress of a particular work dilemma, while a spouse might be more interested in your recent project deadline in relation to upcoming vacation plans. Each of them has a different approach and concern. The business colleague cares about work projects, whereas a spouse may care somewhat about work, such as your job fulfillment, but also cares about household chores, your interpersonal dynamic, certain family affairs, and so on.
Take a moment and think about the different audiences you have in your life and their values and interests. When you speak or interact with them, what are they most concerned about? What matters most to them?

2. Agenda: *Seducing audiences begins before you even open your mouth.*

Once an audience is identified, a celebrity's entourage, such as his or her publicist, manager, or coach, will help the celebrity prepare an agenda. The star is prepped with talking points—key messages that are important to that specific audience. The celebrity has certain key points he or she is prepared to discuss with the media.

There are two key messages to consider: (1) those that relate to the project, such as the film, TV show, or product and (2) those that relate to the likeability and credibility of the actor. Both are important. The actor must market the movie and him or herself. Therefore, the agenda and talking points must follow suit.

The same is true for all of us. When I go into a meeting, what talking points do I need to have in order to be a personal success, convey the desired message about who I am, and address the needs of the work audience? What three key points will make a difference in how I am perceived and what bottom lines are relevant to that audience? Also, what impression or longstanding relationship do I want to build with my colleagues? Do I want them to think of me as a leader or friend? There's no judgment in either, but it's important to think about this beforehand.

Knowing and believing your key messages has to come from your authentic self first. Preparing to talk about them in advance with well thought-out talking points will help get your messages across effectively.

When you only have a few minutes of "airtime" like during an interview in a press setting or making a first impression in a personal or professional setting, expressing your *authentic* point of view, irresistible offer or best self can make or break you. Preparing the talking points you want to convey beforehand helps you communicate them with impact. Knowing and embodying your key messages can get your foot in the door, help you shine when it matters most or allow someone of significance to witness your authentic self.

3. Call to Action: *The desired result you hope to achieve.*

A *call to action* is the expression and deliberate delivery of a specific ask, request, proposal, or *irresistible offer*. In Hollywood Press, we also call this a "plug." The term "plug" is a favorable mention of a current project, such as a film, book, TV show or campaign, and the main reason the celebrity is called for an interview on a talk show, for example.

While other questions are asked of the celebrity, that star's main objective is to raise awareness about his or her project, which is the agenda. However, awareness is not enough. The star must invite or ask people to do something specific about the project.

For example: "Go watch my movie, *Superstars*, which opens on Friday, August 2nd nationwide," or "Buy my book, *Superstar Secrets*, which is now available online at www.mywebsite.com for $15."

A *call to action* can also be an offer, or dare I say, even an *irresistible offer*. For example, a product spokesperson may offer a discount for a certain product. It is used to entice customers to buy the product in hopes of an upsell.

In our personal lives, an *irresistible offer* may be an exceptional overture we extend to another for the sake of building or repairing a relationship. Let's look at one such example.

The Husband

A middle-aged Taiwanese man showed up to a workshop one morning right after an argument with his wife. He walked in and shared with us that the two of them had been at odds with one another off and on for over a year. That morning their ongoing tension boiled over and she told him she wanted a divorce. Hearing that news was a fresh wound, and we could see that he was suffering.

As he continued to share his story, I carefully probed into his pattern of communication. Was he clear and direct with his wife? Could he identify his feelings and the problems he felt were a part of their relationship? He kept trying to defend himself, saying, "But she doesn't get me. She doesn't understand that I am trying."

After listening to him for a while, I asked for female volunteers to do some role-playing with him. The purpose was to give him feedback from a female perspective on how he was communicating with his wife. This would also give him a chance to react or respond to her declaration, a desire for divorce.

What he discovered through that exercise was quite eye opening. The women in the room suggested that what his wife really wanted from him was to be acknowledged and not taken for granted. They claimed she did not want a divorce, but rather, she wanted to be appreciated by him. She wanted to be seen and heard as an equal in the relationship.

Their insights struck a nerve with him. He got defensive, but once he really listened to them, he gained a sense of clarity—he needed to create a new dynamic in their relationship.

After some additional feedback, tears, and reflection, he decided to do something special. What was it? He offered to take his wife out for ice cream. Yes, ice cream. Don't laugh. This unlikely and fun action designed to get both of them out of their usual routine would give him an opportunity—one that he could not do in the heat of an argument—to clearly declare, "I will take you less for granted and commit to doing something with you, out of the house, once a week."

Where did he come up with this idea? The women in the workshop suggested it.

His action was simple, yet powerful. By listening to the women in the room and role-playing, he discovered that a straightforward and uncomplicated action of attention (ice cream) would achieve a different result.

He identified an *irresistible offer*: a commitment to give his wife time and attention—to hear her and be with her. He did not want the divorce, yet did not know how to express his affection and care for her. His declaration, or simple *irresistible offer,* made all the difference. If even for just that one day, this husband took a step: an action that impacted his relationship.

The *call to action* is most often what people overlook when they step into the spotlight. As my friend Ben once said, "Everyone is grabbing for the microphone, yet they don't know what to do once they have it."

What do you do when given an opportunity to speak or heal a situation? Do you take advantage of it? Do you use it to create a desired result or simply fill up the time with air, talking aimlessly without creating change or impact?

The Art of Authentic Promotion in Action

Let's examine how *The A Factor* is exemplified in some of the stories we've looked at so far:

Oprah

Audience: She had two audiences during our interview with her. The first audience was the specific crew and host. The second audience was the target audience of the talk show: stay-at-home moms.

Agenda: Her professional agenda that day was to promote or "plug" her talk show. Her secondary or more personal agenda was to inspire and share her wisdom.

The Call to Action: Be the best person you can be. Don't sit on the sidelines trying to be somebody else. She addressed the host of the talk show directly, yet also spoke through her to the audience at home. As a result, she continued to build her inspiring image and draw in audiences to watch her show.

TEDx Skid Row

Audience: Individuals who were curious about life experiences very different from their own. They wanted to know what it was like on Skid Row and how these men and women transformed their lives. They were looking for inspiration.

Agenda: To share their ideas—to express an idea worth

spreading. They were there to motivate others on how to overcome adversity. The speakers, although most recently on Skid Row, were executives, teachers, and artists— people we would not expect to be homeless.

The Call to Action: The speakers challenged the audience to re-evaluate its perspectives of the homeless population by volunteering for a specific charity. They actually asked people to sign up, there on site, for an upcoming event.

In both of these scenarios, the speakers or presenters— individuals who stepped into the spotlight—drew in their audiences on a personal and direct level. They were clear about what they wanted to accomplish. They prepared in advance—what the husband in the workshop had not done— and thus created change.

Lesson Learned

Be authentic in your communication

When looking at **The A Factor,** consider these powerful questions:

- Are you communicating something extraordinary and tailoring your message to a specific audience?
- Are you clear about what you want to accomplish as the outcome?
- Are you promoting yourself in a unique and memorable way?

Summary

- The *art of authentic promotion* is the ability to communicate and position yourself with clarity to a specific audience.
- **The A Factor** is the core of the *art of authentic promotion*, and consists of three key elements: Agenda, Audience, and Call to Action.
- An *irresistible offer* is a distinct and unique opportunity that comes from a truly extraordinary and authentic place of being.

Exercise

1. Take a look at a recent moment when you were in the spotlight and evaluate it using the three parts of **The A Factor.**
2. Did you clearly know your audience? Had you defined an agenda before speaking?
3. Was there a *call to action* you shared with your audience?
4. I suspect most of you will use an example where you purposefully had to speak or present, such as a work situation or public event. Now challenge yourself and think about a personal example, such as a conflict or a relationship. How does this three-step process work in that type of scenario?

The Call to Action

Prepare for an upcoming spotlight moment. Get clear on what you want to convey. Write out *The A Factor* descriptors. When you are better prepared, your message comes across stronger. How well did you perform?

CHAPTER 7

Clarity in Communication Tool Kit

Five Tips for Creating Clarity

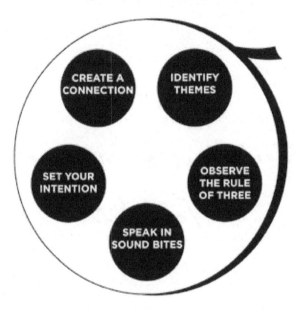

To create clarity in communication and present their best "authentic self," high-profile figures carefully prepare for press interviews and public appearances. The following tips used by celebrities, entertainment executives, media experts, and personality brands can help you with your own self-promotion practices.

Creating Clarity Tip #1: Identify Themes

One of the most powerful and effective communication tools is the art of storytelling. It connects you with an audience, gets your point across, and reinforces it through shared experiences. Stories almost always contain themes that universally touch on the human condition.

For example, often there are themes such as victory,

success, or prosperity, which draw in certain audiences. Others are drawn toward themes of love, compassion, and forgiveness. Themes speak to us personally about our own values and beliefs. When we reveal these themes to others, we share a part of ourselves with them.

Creating Clarity Tip #2: Observe the Rule of Three

The details of a story you will share can be overwhelming, so simply remember there are three parts to *any* story: (1) a beginning, (2) the middle and (3) an end. All you have to remember when you are sharing a story and are trying to connect are these three simple points. If you miss a small detail along the way, that's okay.

Creating Clarity Tip #3: Speak in Sound Bites

The best way to engage others is to leave them wanting more. Others will remember only a fraction of what you say, so make sure to keep your message brief, yet powerful. This means having a 30-second sound bite.

What is a sound bite? It is a stand-alone statement that, even if taken out of context, has integrity and accurately represents your brand, your work, or your public identity. It originated as a journalism term for a piece of an interview that represents what someone is speaking about.

Why are sound bites important? I believe often we are all under the same scrutiny as politicians. For example, in an argument your loved one might say to you, "But you said, 'X Y Z.'"

They are repeating something important you said that stands out to them. They are repeating a sound bite back to you. So why not learn how to speak with integrity-based sound bites from the get-go?

Creating Clarity Tip #4: Set Your Intention

There is no need to act, over explain, or impress anyone. Be willing to lose those who do not value what you have to offer. Chasing them and trying to be everything to everyone dilutes your offer to the point where you will have no impact. Speak to those who want what you have. Set your intention, from the beginning, to hit the heart and value of your target audience.

Creating Clarity Tip #5: Create a Connection

Don't be afraid to share a little bit of yourself. Go beyond the surface. Audiences want a connection. Decide in advance what you are comfortable revealing and create clear boundaries beforehand. Don't allow yourself to get caught up in an awkward situation where you are stumbling on words because you don't know what to say and what not to say. Advance preparation is crucial. Saying nothing personal is not an option, so pick five to ten personal stories and facts that you want to share with others.

SECTION IV:

Confidence

CHAPTER 8

Understanding the Value of the Message

Celebrity Branding Principle: **There are two types of confidence: (1) belief in the value of your message and (2) the "you" that shows up in front of others.**

Now that we have achieved clarity, let's turn to the second "C" of the 3Cs: **Confidence**. We've all heard that the number one fear most people have is public speaking. Why is it so terrifying? We are all public speakers. Every single day, each and every one of us is called to speak, present, and persuade. Whether or not we shine, communicate effectively, or obtain our desired results depends upon our confidence.

As a media coach, I help people present themselves to all kinds of media. The most widely used media are broadcast, digital, print, and online channels. There is also a medium that exists live, in person, and in real-time. It is you. Yes, each and every one of us is a medium of communication. We communicate in front of audiences all the time.

From the moment we begin to interact with others, we learn how to address an audience.

While we know how to communicate, we may not always be confident. This is especially true when we are the subjects, when we have to talk about ourselves.

Many of us can talk about a product, a belief, or business at great length because we know the subject matter quite well. For example, we know how to talk about our business at a pitch meeting or about our products at a trade show. We can freely express and promote the value of a "thing."

Can we do the same for ourselves? Not always.

There are times when we speak to an audience of one— our individual selves. Each of us has an internal exchange that sets the tone for all outward communication. This is called self-talk. It is that voice inside that speaks to you. At times it is an internal motivator that shouts, "Go out there and do your best!" Other times, it is a whisper that instills self-doubt. It's a powerful conversation.

As a coach, I've often witnessed that the loudest voice we

hear is self-defeating dialogue. For example, we might say, "I can't. I won't. I shouldn't."

While this may seem to be the start of a private, intimate conversation, it sets up our communication with others. This dialogue formulates our views, ideas, and notions of the world that we then, one way or another, express to others. As parents, professionals, friends, spouses, and entrepreneurs, that internal dialogue can say we may not be quite on par with others. We identify as "less than."

When our self-talk is negative, it is hard to see that we truly have value. We go down a road where we feel we "have to" compensate for a lack of something, such as education, height, looks, or past success.

We might get sidetracked by the self-sabotaging internal dialogue of "I can't." This can include "I can't compete," or "I am not as good" or "I have to change." What's worse is we project this sense of "less than" to others and they begin to believe that about us.

We have to shift the belief of our innate value. When we shift internal conflicts between knowing we have innate value and *believing* it, then we can positively identify ourselves as a business or a brand—and get into the art of authentic self-promotion.

The underlying questions that come up when we are called to self-promote are: "Am I good enough? Do I have value?"

If we can't grasp the internal dialogue of "I can't," it will always affect how we see ourselves with others and in understanding our value in relation to others.

When we speak about ourselves, we need not believe what other people have told us, either about our own story or the way we are expected to be. "Have to be" and "should be" are the enemies of confidence. As parents, for example, we may have an internal dialogue that reflects, "I shouldn't" or "I need to," such as "I shouldn't allow my son to behave this way" or "I need to be stricter." Instead, think of how you can be the best you for your child. Being authentic matters, especially as a person of influence.

Some people hold on to the notion that showing up a certain way—such as holding your head up or using hand gestures—means you have confidence. To me, without truly understanding and believing in the value of the message, all you are doing is sharpening your acting skills.

Using body gestures and "proper" speaking mechanics in the right context can show confidence. But without truly believing in the message, you don't hit the confidence mark completely. Your actions are empty.

Have you ever heard someone speak in front of a room and all you heard was, "Blah, blah, blah?" In those instances, we are being spoken to. The speaker is not truly connecting with us, nor are we connecting with the speaker.

How many times have you seen an individual get in front of a room and do a presentation flawlessly? He or she hit all the points precisely, knew what the audience needed, and how his or her product fit those needs. However, connecting has to be authentic. I've seen a person do a flawless sales presentation for a product. Yet, when it comes to self-promotion, such as a job interview, networking event, or first date, that same individual may completely miss the mark, failing to connect the audience's need to the real product, which is the individual as a person. Instead he or she projects who they "think" they should be, thereby missing a real connection.

Connection has a direct link to confidence. When you are called to step into the spotlight in any arena, personally or professionally, you are presenting yourself, your thoughts, or ideas in front of people—real human beings. Those human beings have real emotions. If you are on a stage and are speaking *at* them, then you are performing. You are doing a monologue. You are reading a script. You are not engaging them.

Your audience—whether it is just one person or several—has emotions, desires, wants, and fears. What you are speaking about touches all of these core human elements. Connection is the ability to put yourself in someone else's shoes, to see things from his or her vantage point, and know that you, yourself, have those same experiences. It is relating to another human being on a basic level. It is based on empathy, appreciation, and understanding.

The Web Designer

When I first started doing communication workshops in Asia, I noticed immediately the number of participants who presented themselves with great physical awareness. Many of them also exhibited wonderful speaking skills. Many Asian professionals are poised showmen. They make eye contact, stand tall, and smile. Paul, the web designer, was one such individual. By all appearances, he and others like him are confident. But are they really? Not necessarily.

These professionals are merely projecting an image they believe others want to see. They rely on this fulfilled expectation to make an impression. This established norm makes almost everyone the same—to the point where nobody shines. There is nothing unique in how they show up as individuals. They lack an authentic connection with others.

Confidence is not grounded in fulfilling an expected role.

Embodying your best self showcases it.

Paul's goal was to give the impression that he is in control of his message. When he came up to speak during our workshop, he showed up with a very professional posture. This appearance of confidence, however, lacked something to back it up. It lacked a connection. He struggled with his *irresistible offer*, something that his clients could not get from anybody else. He could not pinpoint what made him unique and special.

In marketing, this is called a *unique value proposition (UVP)*. Your *UVP* is that special niche you've carved out in the marketplace that sets you apart. Paul found it easy to talk about why his service was good, but he could not identify what made it an extraordinary opportunity for respective clients.

A martial arts expert, he knew how to physically be present with strength, yet he knew innately that this was not enough to attract clients. He was in a creative space, but simply projecting a "strong" determined person did not build confidence in his clients. He was not connecting to their needs. He was merely showcasing a professional demeanor.

During our coaching time together, Paul started to break down what his clients might need from him. He identified their fear of technology, their desire to have a digital storefront that accurately represented their business, and a passion to co-create a domain with someone who exemplified collaboration. They would hire him if he showed up comprehensively, which meant he needed to connect with their needs and present an *irresistible offer*. What did this look like for him? It showed up in Paul's natural passionate, caring, and enthusiastic demeanor. He, however, did not showcase these attributes when he first met with his clients.

After we identified what the clients might need, we took time to delve deeper into a skill that all of us can use when we have to be present and connect with others. That skill was to listen. Being better listeners can help us be better, more effective speakers. It shows our confidence in being able to connect with others and their needs.

One way to do this is through *active listening*. This skill helps deepen **The A Factor** formula by breaking down the specific needs of your audience. It requires you to listen deeply for what is not being expressed but that you can hopefully understand, such as an underlying emotion or concern. The following chart offers examples for practicing active listening.

Audience	Need or Want	Emotion	How to Make a Connection
Web Clients	• Create a distinct website for my business • Stand out in the marketplace	• Fear of not getting it right • Failure to find collaborative designer	• Repeat what I've heard • Show visual examples of what I've heard • Validate their concerns and show my approach
Prospective Boss	• Find the right candidate with skills and compatibility	• Concern about finding the right mix, being fooled, bringing in the wrong person	• Showcase not only my skills, but find similarities in approach and personality • Validate need to find the right match
Networking Event Participants	• Meet new people, new collaboration, potential work partners	• Fear of wasting time, being awkward, not connecting, being fake	• Ask about his or her interests for commonalities, show intere • Relax—don't be too concerned about trying to impress

In each of these examples, making a connection involves validating what is being heard or addressed by your audience. You understand, empathize, and appreciate the other person or people. You make a connection. You are confident in what you have to offer. This shows up not because you are fulfilling a role, but because you are offering something that is uniquely you. You are offering your best self... and there's no better way to show confidence.

Now what happens when your confidence or belief in

yourself is challenged or tarnished by either real-life events or gossip? Let's look at one such example. The bankrupt performer showed up with grace and connected with me in a way that I will always remember and appreciate.

The Bankrupt Performer

Part of my job as a producer was to interview celebrities. Sometimes these were at junkets and press conferences. Other times, they were booked as separate sit-down interviews at a hotel or private office. Every now and then I sat with personalities I loved and adored. This performer was one of them.

After having a few hit singles, being awarded Grammys and several other awards, she ran into some financial troubles. So even being in the spotlight with the biggest hit of her career, she dropped out of the public eye and wasn't seen for quite some time.

My friend and colleague, Shahnti Olcese Brook, was the music producer for *TV Guide Channel*. We were the team that traveled the U.S. interviewing TV stars, film actors, and music artists. Shahnti knew how much I loved this artist, so she invited me to do the interview.

I was a little anxious at first, something that didn't happen too often, but now and then came on me like a bad flu. We drove out to a Beverly Hills hotel and set up the shoot in one of the suites. While we waited, I reviewed my interview questions, thinking mostly about her music, but also giving some thought to her personal setback.

When she walked in, she was so gracious and wonderful. Her publicist, on the other hand, seemed uptight, and rightfully so, because this was the artist's first interview in over a year.

She and I connected right away. What was supposed to be a fifteen-minute interview turned into one that lasted more than an hour. She definitely had a lot to say, and most of it had to do with her career, her upbringing, and what lay ahead. When the moment came to address her financial setbacks, she thought for a moment and said something like, "You know, for those who wondered where I've been, I've taken time to get my life together. What's important now is that I am back. No setback is going to keep me down. Life happens to all of us, and if I can pick myself up with all that has happened in my life—the various struggles I've faced from bad relationships to business decisions—you can do it, too. I am here to make music and my fans happy."

I don't think I could have crafted a better response. She addressed the issue and took it to a positive place. I call this *tap and go*. Essentially, it is the ability to address the question and *take it to a positive place*, all the time staying connected to and respected by the audience. She knew her audience and what they wanted. As much as Hollywood (and many of us) enjoys a scandal, we also love a comeback story.

Why do we love comeback stories? I'd like to believe it hits on a core human experience—that we all fail at times, but we can redeem ourselves and make our lives even better than before.

She embodied confidence in her work as a music artist and public personality. She didn't avoid talking about what happened, but didn't let it become a bigger issue than necessary. She also connected with her audience on a personal level. She told her brief experience and brought it back to something they, ultimately, wanted to know... that she would again bring them great entertainment and beautiful music. This is something that she did and continues to do for her audience.

To button up this experience was a true surprise that I did not expect. The day after the interview—the very next day—I got a surprise phone call from her. She actually tracked me down at my office to express her appreciation. This is the one and only time a celebrity has sought me out in this way to say thank you. What an amazing way to show poise, class, and gratitude.

And So?

Respect your audience and they will respect you. We all have shared human experiences. That means you are like your audience—one among them—not apart from them. At the same, your star shines when you inspire, motivate, and transform your audience. Part of being a celebrity in your everyday life is being able to touch and connect with that other human being across from you. There is a wonderful dynamic: you are just like that person, however you have something exceptional to share with them.

You're not performing as an actor reading a script, but as a person who is exceptional because you have touched and moved people. The movement can be big or small, but it is always significant. The instant when it happens is that moment when you step into the spotlight.

For example, when an executive interviews for a new position, a mom guides her child, or when a teen makes a new friend, they are all reaching out to another person in hopes of creating an honest and powerful interaction. They ultimately want to impact that person and react in a certain way. In all of these situations, there is a connection between two or more people.

The conviction you have in your subject matter shows confidence. How well do you identify and know your best self? If you get caught up in "should be" or "have to be" a certain way, then how can your true, authentic, and exceptional self connect with others? How can you WOW your audience?

Lesson Learned

Know your true value and be willing to share it

One surefire way to identify your best self and clarify your *irresistible offer* as an everyday celebrity is to objectify yourself. Identify your personal brand. See yourself as a product, just like celebrities do. Look at yourself in third person so your emotional baggage—negative self-talk and the self-doubt that you've built through the years—disappears. See yourself not in the way others have defined you, or how you "should be," but how you really are.

Summary

- The first component of **confidence** is the belief in your message. It is the undeniable truth that your subject matter has value.
- This understanding is key to self-promotion. Sharing our true and authentic selves connects real value or significance to our audience.
- Part of making a connection with people involves actively listening to them.
- Getting to the bottom of negative self-beliefs, damaging self-talk, and the "should be" and "have to be" chatter in your head is a crucial step toward building confidence.

Exercise

Here's a little help in objectifying yourself in a positive way. It's what I like to call a bio exercise.

1. Take a sheet of paper and fold it in half.
2. On the left-hand side write down five different accomplishments you have achieved in your life so far. They can be personal, like marrying the love of your life, having children, or graduating from college. They can also be professional, such as becoming a manager or starting your own business. After you've done this, put it down and walk away, anywhere from fifteen minutes to a day.
3. Look at the right-hand column and add some quantifying measures to your accomplishment. For example, next to graduating from college you can write, "While working a 40-hour-a-week job and raising two kids."
4. After filling in these two columns, fold it up and again take a little time to walk away from it.
5. After a little time has passed, pick up the paper, open it, and read it.
6. Then on the backside write a bio about the person who did all these things. Write it in third person using these five accomplishments as your "facts." Try not to put too much opinion in it. Be as objective as possible.
7. Then, read it. If you are feeling adventurous, read it aloud to a friend. See if "that person on paper" (the real you in facts) is the person who shows up in real life (your public image). Are you confidently showing up to others with your best self? See how they respond to it. Do they connect to you?

The Call to Action

See yourself through a new lens—one that focuses on your true story of success. Is this what you share with others? If not, why? It's real.

CHAPTER 9

The "You" That Shows Up

Celebrity Branding Principle: **Confidence shows up when you use your entire being and body as a tool of self-expression.**

I've been told that my work centers on instilling confidence in others. I believe this is largely true. However, confidence requires more than just mechanics, such as the pitch of your voice, body gestures, and prepared message points. Your knowledge of the subject matter and its relevance to your audience is another significant element to exuding confidence.

Confidence shows up in your entire being. Confidence requires your mind, body, and soul. When they are aligned and in agreement, you can be convincing, powerful, and certain. You can also be deliberate, compassionate, and dynamic. In essence, you can be confident.

One way you show up confidently is by being an expert in your subject matter, whether the subject is you, your work, or your beliefs. The "you" that shines under the spotlight stands with certainty that what you are talking about is valuable and relevant. When you go to a convention, you witness this expertise in most presenters or keynote speakers. They demonstrate determination in their convictions because they are experts in that domain. They embody celebrity essence. They show up like a celebrity in front of a room.

Using your voice, facial expressions, eyes, posture, and gestures in concert as a tool of self-expression is a huge part of capturing an audience. Showing up with the right attitude and demeanor in the right situation for the proper audience is a skill that can be practiced and learned.

Context is another important consideration in communication. In addition to knowing your audience, take into account the environment and setting. Knowing the context in which to show assertiveness versus compassion, wit versus seriousness, or other contradictory approaches also impacts your effectiveness in the spotlight.

You can step into the spotlight with a contradictory personal energy that will minimize your ability to connect and show your value to an audience. For example, a sad and emotional story may not be the best icebreaker on a first date at an amusement park, or students telling jokes during a disciplinary review is probably not the best way to avoid punishment.

While these examples may be very obvious, there are smaller nuances that quite often appear in everyday situations. Some contextual items to consider in a communication exchange include:

- Demographic breakdown of your audience—Age, sex, ethnic background, income
- Mood of your audience—Are they happy, upset, motivated?
- Purpose of the exchange—Similar to an agenda, this indicates why people are giving you their attention. Are you at a town hall meeting? A first date? An interview?
- Medium—Are you on camera? In person? On the phone? On video conference?

All of these factors give you the speaker or presenter, important details to determine the best way to approach a situation. Paying attention to the context can better equip you to enter that particular spotlight moment with greater certainty and determine the most appropriate personal approach. It's important to note, however, that this does not mean you have to be anything other than who you are authentically. Rather it helps you decide what part of your best self to call forward.

Experts and Powerful Presence

Experts who are seasoned and skilled at what they do, such as doctors, police officers, and teachers, embody a certain form of confidence. They stand as professionals in a specific field and exude a presence that is undeniable. Looking at them, you can see they are the real deal. Whether they have other stories floating in their heads remains to be seen externally, but for all intents and purposes, they show up in a notable fashion.

Part of my media coaching work, in both TV and other professional settings, is to help transform subject-matter experts into professional media personalities, whether that means getting up in front of a room, promoting themselves in social media, or being on broadcast TV. Among the many folks that I've had the pleasure to work with have been interior designers, scientists, motivational speakers, and even fiction writers.

At the *International Women's Fiction Festival* in Matera, Italy, I received a big reaction when I asserted that each author is an expert. They *are* experts—as storytellers, queens of romance, and masters of character development. When they were called to step into the spotlight in an interview or conference presentation, they often saw themselves as "just writers," not experts.

One talented author named Sally opened her eyes wide when this realization hit her. Before my exchange, I don't think she ever saw her value as anything more than a writer. She even shared that she escaped into storytelling because it allowed her to be somebody else. At this conference, up until a private coaching moment, she was not seen. She hid. Our brief exchange gave her a moment to step into her own personal spotlight. All it took was a personal connection in which she was challenged to see herself in a new way: where someone took the time to validate her expertise and talent.

Sally recognized her own value and showed up

confidently—she stood differently, walked assuredly, and spoke powerfully. Was it I who made this difference? No, absolutely not. I merely represented an audience that she respected. I was a celebrity expert who reflected back her own celebrity presence.

I have had the privilege to see this sort of positive physical energy in a variety of different ways and with different people. I produced a sit-down interview with Sylvester Stallone. While I wasn't the interviewer, I witnessed how he walked into the room, larger than life, addressed all of us, and radiated physical presence. He sauntered in as a professional. He was an expert at being an action star and it showed.

Another example of confident energy that I experienced was when I interviewed Evander Holyfield, a world-famous boxer. While backstage at an award show, I was a little nervous to meet him, since I am not particularly athletic myself. When he walked in and sat in the chair across from me, I saw this large man who was poised and impeccably dressed. He had positive energy that seemed to pour out of him.

What was the first question I asked him? I asked about his shoes. Yep, that was the first thing that came out of my mouth. I could see that they were expensive and that he or his stylist paid careful attention in selecting them. I suspected that being well dressed made him feel good. This well-known, popular athlete took the time to look sharp and I appreciated it. I wanted to honor that and connect with him on that level. He was very receptive and this made the rest of the interview more relaxed and comfortable. Evander Holyfield presented himself powerfully and confidently and, surprisingly, connected with me over an unlikely yet relatable subject—shoes.

Powerful energy is not limited to action stars and world-class athletes. We all have it. Sally showed it. I've seen it in many clients from executives to child actors to creative professionals. Every one of them showed up as true experts in their field. You can, too.

Why is being an expert important? When we experience experts, we immediately respect and admire them. Experts have authority. They show up in a commanding and determined fashion. They walk and speak with ease about their skills, position, and purpose. Their passion is apparent. We see it in their eyes, gestures, and body posture. Even if they are a little awkward or shy, there is no doubt about their commitment to their craft.

Passion and commitment show up visibly in all of us. Together these two elements reveal the physical manifestation of confidence. It is an outward expression of an internal conviction that audience members experience.

All of us are experts, one way or another. You don't have to be an actor, scientist, professional athlete, or TV host to stand with power and determination. You can be a friend, spouse, or citizen, and be an expert at it.

What holds us back? Fear. Simply put, we are scared to stand with courage and conviction behind our passion. We lack the commitment to try, make mistakes, and try again and again. Sound ironic?

Not really. An expert takes advantage of opportunity and experience to improve, learn, and once again look at things with open eyes. In many ways, an expert is the constant student, the perpetual new beginner.

The Visual Stylist Turned TV Correspondent

Many of the programs I've worked on as a producer and coach

were lifestyle-based talk shows. These kinds of shows focus on a range of self-improvement and how-to topics. They cover an array of subject matter from how to be a better lover or parent to cooking the perfect meal or redesigning your home. One of the most popular segments on these programs is beauty: how to sharpen your style, get the perfect eyebrows, or cut your hair to complement your face. This includes makeovers—an all-time favorite for many viewers. Imagine seeing a visual transformation that can change someone's life. It's powerful television.

I was hired onto one of these lifestyle-based talk shows in San Francisco to coach a veteran visual stylist on how to be a TV correspondent. A "visual stylist" is a well-known entertainment term used to describe someone who can do makeup, hair, and fashion. Specifically, this professional knows how to make sure all three of these elements are visually perfect for video, print, and digital images. It's like the triple threat of beauty for the triple threat of media. The visual stylist I worked with was, indeed, all that and then some.

Amy was superb at her job. She was seasoned and had made countless celebrities, politicians, performers. and TV personalities look their best. She knew exactly what was needed and how to enhance someone's natural style. She did this in the most direct way possible. And by direct, I mean *direct*. She did not hold back yet, at the same time, had a kind, compassionate and supportive nature. It is rare to find someone who can pull off that kind of approach. That is exactly why she was hired on this program.

My job was to transform her into a TV correspondent: to pull out her natural charm and tailor it for broadcast. This meant refining her approach just enough so she could do her magic in a compressed amount of time that would keep TV viewers interested in seeing the results. It also meant to help her show people how to do it themselves.

Amy was an expert visual stylist. She had presence. She was confident in her expertise, but not as an expert TV correspondent.

Our challenge, hers to accomplish and mine to coach her through, was to fine-tune her expertise for a specific audience. She was tasked to connect with them, uncover their needs, and equip them with useful and practical expertise. For years she worked with high-profile personalities who were accustomed to her candor and directness.

TV audiences, however, were not.

At first this rattled her. She was called to be in front of the camera, when she had spent an entire career behind it. She knew firsthand what it took to be good on TV. But that was exactly the point. We weren't trying to make her a different person. Our mission was for her to connect with the TV audience. This meant showcasing her assertive personality and value as an expert.

At first Amy stumbled. She didn't come off as a fine-tuned version of herself. She took on some of the "have to be" and "should be" attributes that she thought would make her valuable to the audience. This is natural.

Many—and I mean many of the people I've worked with through the years—take on this attitude. They try to change their personalities and presentation styles to fit what they believe the audience expects. Being on TV or speaking in front of a room rattles them. The new environment or setting creates pressure for them. Yet, whether it's one person or an audience of several hundred people, the goal is the same: *be yourself.*

Amy's lack of confidence as a TV correspondent did not last too long. She embraced being a learner. She understood she was a novice in a new arena. She welcomed the opportunity to better herself and learned the art of being a media personality. Like a true professional expert, she sought to improve her skill set, and for this courage, I will always admire her. She faced her fears and became an excellent on-camera commentator.

Lesson Learned

Confidence requires your mind, body and soul

When your entire being is aligned and in agreement, you are powerful and effective. You show your confidence. It is felt and seen. For example, your conviction is witnessed in your eyes and felt by your audience. Passion is revealed through your gestures, rhythm of speech, and your facial expressions, which are mirrored by those who see you. When you smile, they smile.

Confidence begins inside. Courage allows the world to see it. For courage connects the two elements of confidence: (1) belief in the value of your message and (2) the "you" that shows up in front of others, which has to be authentic.

Be courageous. Be confident.

Summary

- You are your own expert. Learn how to speak with ease about your unique skills, position, and purpose.
- Passion and commitment show up physically. They are visible and noticeable.
- Understanding context is essential for effective communication. It allows you to determine the best and most appropriate approach for a given situation and audience.

Exercise

1. Take a look at a recent personal spotlight moment, such as a networking event, town hall meeting, date, or conflict.
2. List the different elements that shaped the context of the exchange. For example, was it on the phone or in person? Did you know the person well or was this a new relationship?
3. Were you aware of how these elements might shape or inform you how to best communicate with that individual/audience?
4. Looking back, how might you have approached the exchange differently? Consider in what ways you showed up as an "expert," be it an expert spouse, friend, or employee, for example. In that expert role, were you your best self?

The Call to Action

Confidence is built on knowing what you have to say is valuable to your audience. One can appear self-assured, but in order to really make an impact, it's important to actually be internally resolute about your irresistible offer. What steps can you take to make sure you know what's special and unique about you?

CHAPTER 10

Confidence in Communication Tool Kit

Five Tips for Building Confidence

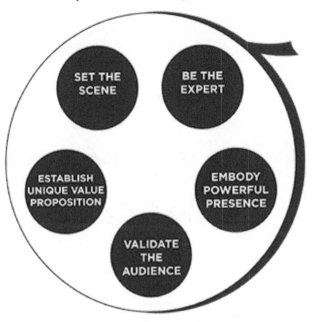

When high-profile figures prepare for press interviews and public appearances, they have a toolkit they can draw from, so they always look cool, calm, and collected. Here are five tips that help build confidence and your star power foundation.

Building Confidence Tip #1: Be the Expert

An audience is looking to you for information. Accept it. Embrace it. What you want others to know is up to you. Don't assume they know who you are, what you have to offer, or what you're talking about. Give them a little insight into your world, new information about something interesting, or "how to" material they can use. They will love you. Share your value and expertise generously with others.

Building Confidence Tip #2: Embody Powerful Presence

Do not get caught up in words. If it feels like a rehearsed speech where you have to hit every single phrase or word, it most likely will come across that way to your audience—your body will show it. You will contract and hold back your natural internal energy. Even the subtlest differences in your body can cue your audience that you missed a point or that you are not on track. Instead, focus on key messages. Your body will show up exactly as it needs to; you will be in the moment and it will show. Others will respond to your internal and external energy. You will be more powerful focusing on messages and not the exact words.

It is crucial to believe with certainty the importance of your contributions before you can speak about them.

Building Confidence Tip #3: Validate the Audience

Empathy in action. That's what draws in audiences. They want to know you understand and appreciate them, their perspective, and their circumstances. In doing so, you connect one human to another. When they see an actor in a role, they see him as that character and empathize with that human experience. Likewise, your everyday audience wants to see a part of themselves in you. You can validate their experience and existence.

Building Confidence Tip #4: Establish Your Unique Value Proposition (UVP)

What sets you apart? Get past the "should be" and "have to be" mentality. You are a star with particular value, but if you don't know your worth, nobody else will, either.

Look at yourself as a product and isolate what truly sets you apart. Is it your skills, talents, or personal approach? What authentic qualities do you have that stand out from the rest?

Put into words the impact you—and only you—can have on your desired audience. Establish your unique value and show it. In marketing, this is known as a *unique value proposition:* the irresistible offer that sets you apart from others. Be able to answer why the audience should give you their time and attention. Like businesses, knowing your special qualities and worth helps you better market or self-promote.

Building Confidence Tip #5: Set the Scene

Many elements set the scene for a communication exchange, whether it is a presentation, interview, or personal interaction. We create distinctions about our audiences and what they may value. Likewise, we create an impression on our audience, whether that is an audience of one or of many.

We assess one another based on our appearances and physical attributes. We communicate non-verbally who we are and what we value (as a speaker and receiver) just by being present in the room or situation. Sometimes these accurately represent us. Other times they misrepresent our intentions. Therefore, we need to be aware of them and embrace them as part of the overall message. These nonverbal, physical cues include:

- Body: Posture, body language, position
- Profile: Sex, age, income, appearance
- Emotion: Your personal mood, as well as that of the room
- Eyes: Eyes and facial impressions reveal your thoughts and feelings

All of these create a context to help us communicate better. For example, if you see a 60-year-old man in a suit with his arms crossed glaring at you in a conference room, you will likely approach him differently than you would a trendy 22-year-old female sales associate in fashionable attire waving at you in a department store. By assessing the environment and individuals in your audience, you can gauge your information and message to help you show up more confidently.

SECTION V:

Charisma

CHAPTER 11

Unleashing Your Best Self

Celebrity Branding Principle: **Charisma is the ability to fully engage an audience with your unique and authentic being.**

It is a commonly held belief in the entertainment business that celebrities sponsor stars on the *Hollywood Walk of Fame* or, to put it more bluntly, they pay for them. The implication that you can buy star power is provocative. I believe *star quality* is something we all have, not only the celebrities with stars on Hollywood Boulevard. You can't buy it. You can't bargain to be a star. Star power is in you.

You already have star power: special, authentic, and unique characteristics that shine. The challenge is how you tap into those star qualities.

Do you dare place a star on your own personal *Hollywood Walk of Fame*? Or, do you choose to see only those stars around you? If so, you are denying a gift that can transform, heal, move, direct, lighten, ground, or have endless possibilities for others. Identifying, nurturing, and showcasing the specialness of your being and personality make up the third "C": *Charisma.*

We often believe that charisma is being charming, sophisticated, or elaborate. Charisma is your delivery style and natural way of promoting yourself and your personal brand. It is your best way of communicating, using your innate skills, and bringing them out so you can connect with another person clearly and confidently. Charisma requires commitment and consistency. It is your repeated style of expression. For some, it is humor; for others, it is drama. Sometimes, it is directness; other times, it is sarcasm.

Charisma is:
- the fashion in which you communicate impactful messages
- how you draw in, attract and engage your audience
- how you inspire, motivate, mobilize or transform
- the manifestation of being an everyday celebrity

However, charisma is not limited by these descriptions. Charisma is dynamic. You shine so that others can be moved in some way. At its core, charisma is your human influence, your sparkle, your magic. To illustrate this point, let's look at the strong and the mighty.

The Strong and Mighty

I've had the honor of witnessing two wonderful examples of charisma. Both were huge, high-profile figures, yet they were uniquely different. The first was larger than life in demeanor and the second was a quiet force. Despite their distinct personalities, both were strong and mighty.

The first I met during my tenure as a producer of *Celebrity Profiles*. This funny man was one of the biggest international actors I had met. I fondly remember that spring afternoon when my team and I were setting up for the interview. We were all prepared for this wild and wacky character to storm excitedly into the room, do his thing, entertain us, and quickly depart. Quite the opposite happened.

This actor, who first gained fame as a loony outer space alien on American TV, walked into the conference room with his shoulders down, soft eyes straight ahead, and a simple smile on his face. He didn't say a word at first. He was quiet, almost shy. He circled the room, approached everyone, reached out his hand and with a low-key, "Hello," said to each of us, "Nice to meet you." He then sat down, asked the cameraman if he had the shot he needed, and waited for the interview.

Then it happened. The camera turned on, my fellow producer threw out the first question and Robin Williams was "on" in all his witty and dramatic glory. He was marvelous.

136

He had animated gestures, popped out of his seat, and impersonated popular character voices. It was one of the funniest and most entertaining interviews I've ever been a part of. His charisma, which I identify as witty, dramatic, and clever, showed up in a big way. He engaged us with his own unique star quality.

After the interview was over, he smiled, made one more joke, looked at the interviewer and asked, "Do you have what you need?"

He wanted to make sure she and the audience she represented got the answers to the questions they wanted. He wanted to make sure he delivered them with his own personal brand of humor. He was the master of this spotlight moment. He moved us with laughter and grounded us with thought-provoking stories.

The second strong and mighty person I witnessed was also someone who surprised me. It was early in my career. I was a talent assistant and my role was to greet guests, take them into the green room, which is a hospitality room for celebrities, and tend to their needs before they were interviewed.

I loved meeting fascinating individuals in that job. Celebrities of all sorts came through the studio doors onto that news desk and entertained us. I had the chance to see, hear, meet, and interact with them firsthand.

This celebrity was different. On the day of her interview I was particularly excited because she was not an actress or performer. She was an activist. In fact, many have credited her for being the key figure that helped launch the U.S. Civil Rights movement of the 1960s. At this point, she was obviously much older. It had been decades since, as a young woman, she had done one simple—yet not so simple—act. She had chosen to sit in the front of a public bus. At that time, African-Americans were supposed to sit in the back of the bus, but on that day, this woman chose not to do the status quo.

She was Rosa Parks.

I am honored to have met this historical figure before she died. She left me with a lasting impression because she—who did what many considered a bold act—was not "bold" in personality. She was a quiet force who looked you right in the eye, grinned, and pulled you in with magnetism that was silent but strong. I loved hearing her speak. She was intentional, kind, and articulate.

When I greeted her I said, "It is an honor to meet you." Her reply was, "And it's an honor to meet you. What's your name?"

After introductions, we continued to chat the entire time before they called her to the set. For every question I asked her about her life, she asked me one about mine. I felt like I was talking to my neighbor—a soft-spoken, understated, and gracious neighbor. When it came time for her interview, I walked her onto the set, and she turned around and asked if she would see me afterward.

I replied, "Yes," and she said, "Good."

During the course of her interview I sat back and saw the same woman I experienced backstage; she was gracious, kind, and focused. She was calm, centered, and spoke in a soft, yet deliberate, tone. She indicated during her interview that the day she took a stand against injustice wasn't necessarily planned. She simply had put up with enough prejudice and decided she wasn't going to take it any longer. She was in the moment then and continued to be "in the moment" when I met her.

Even though Robin Williams and Rosa Parks each had their own style of engagement, they both came across as authentic and genuine. Both of them had their own unique magnetism that drew me in quickly. It was undeniable.

Robin Williams and Rosa Parks each had their own individual attractive force.

This individual kind of charisma is magical. It's what draws people to you, makes you stand out, makes people listen.

The same is true for each of us. Funny, larger-than-life characteristics don't make someone charismatic. Soft-spoken, yet deliberate and kind demeanors do not make someone charismatic. It boils down to authenticity.

Charisma is expressed differently in each of us. Your charisma lies in your own specialness and innate attractive characteristics.

Too often we believe that being charismatic means being attention-grabbing, loud, or entertaining. That's not the case. Being a good speaker, presenter, or celebrity doesn't require you to be an extrovert. You can be shy, reserved, or even insecure, as we all are at times, but know what to do when the spotlight is on you. Being prepared in advance when the metaphorical microphone is handed to you makes all the difference in the world.

We build personal brands when we are committed to what we reveal, how we show up, and the way in which we connect to our audience. Being consistent in these communication behaviors builds expectations and accountability over time.

The term "accountability" scares many of us. We get nervous when others expect that we show up in a certain way, so the key here is tapping into your organic, true, and authentic way of being.

For example, if you try to be funny and tell jokes in front of your friends all the time, you are establishing the groundwork that they can expect you to show up like that most of the time. When you decide to get serious they may not know how to react to you. If you are always accommodating other people's requests at work to the point of never speaking your mind, you are setting the foundation that your needs are not important. You've set an expectation that may leave you unfulfilled and resentful.

Consistency and commitment are not traps. They are opportunities. We can vary and should show a range of ourselves, but people connect best with others when they've identified a personal brand promise.

A personal brand promise in this context means a way of interacting with your audience where you are consistent in what you offer them. They know your unique value proposition (UVP) or *irresistible offer* and can expect you to show up like that consistently.

Think of the friend you always go to when you need to talk or the parent you went to when you needed a certain answer. In both examples, a brand promise was identified and fulfilled. You sought out those people because you experienced them in a consistent and committed fashion.

Look at popular personality brands like Oprah or Lady Gaga. We know what to expect and, in return, they deliver. It is important, however, that when we look at these examples we remember that authenticity is important. You can only fake it for so long. It's tiring and the real truth is—it's not fun.

Lesson Learned

Audiences want something real and authentic

Each of us has an innate demeanor and way of being, and when we show it, we are being charismatic. Don't fake it. We long for sincerity. We live in a world that is too transparent to pretend to be somebody else. If you are in control of your message and your public brand, then you have to be consistent in what you present. If you contradict what you've already established to be your *celebrity essence* and your personal brand, the audience will lose trust in you. Therefore, be prepared and sincere in your communication. The best strategy is an honest one.

Summary

- Charisma is your consistent and committed style of self-promotion. It is based on your authentic, powerful, and unique personality characteristics.
- Being charismatic does not require you to be an extrovert. How you show up as your best self—be it quietly or loudly—is all that matters.
- People connect best with others when they've identified that individual's brand promise—a way of interacting where you are consistent in what you offer.

Exercise

1. Identify two of your favorite celebrities or well-known figures who show up consistently with their *irresistible offer*. They can be actors, performers, athletes, politicians, or other well-known people.
2. What is their *unique value proposition* (UVP)?
3. What three characteristics can you consistently expect from them? How do these characteristics show up? Is it in what they say, how they say it, or what they do?
4. Next, identify two people in your own immediate life, such as a friend, boss, relative, or associate. Ask the same questions as above.

The Call to Action

By identifying the unique value proposition (UVP) of others and the consistency in which it shows up, you can get a better sense of your own. Do you have an irresistible offer that others come to expect from you? How does it show up?

CHAPTER 12

Thriving in the Communication Cycle

Celebrity Branding Principle: **Contextual communication is the most effective form of communication.**

When clients are preparing to give a talk or presentation, I often hear comments like:

- "It's so much harder speaking to a group."
- "I am great one-on-one."
- "It's not the same."

They fear they are not going to be heard or understood. They are concerned that the audience will not be able to respond to them in the same way an individual does in a one-on-one conversation, but the truth is we *do* get feedback anytime we communicate.

Various cues we get from our audience inform and help shape further interaction. The only limitation is our own perspective of the exchange and whether or not we fully embrace the basic communication dynamic present in every exchange (see diagram below). When the context changes, we get anxious, nervous, and sometimes paralyzed.

When we speak to large audiences, present ourselves on-camera, or communicate with a group, they give us feedback and we can respond to it. What does that feedback look like? Sometimes it's direct: eyes wander, smiles lighten up, or heads nod. An audience's body language indicates a true connection, or lack thereof, to our material and to us. We can see if they are engaged, distracted, bored, and ultimately whether or not they value what we are saying—but only if we are paying attention to their reaction.

Sometimes feedback is not visible immediately, but it becomes clear later. The feedback shows up in whether or not the "call to action"—the desired outcome—is achieved or lost. It shows up in a black-and-white "yes" or "no."

For example, how do you know if someone on a date likes

you? He or she goes out with you again. How do you know if a panel liked your speech? They ask questions, seek more information or come up to you afterward. How do you know if you made the sale? There is a purchase.

In all of these communication dynamics, whether they occur one-on-one or in group situations, the results do or do not take place as a result of the exchange or pitch. These results are feedback.

To quickly recap, feedback from others is seen in two ways: (1) facial expressions, body gestures, and the emotions we intuit from our audience, and (2) the results that are generated through the exchange. The feedback we receive helps reinforce our communication tactics. If we make the sale, then we are likely to do the same pitch next time. If we do not, our natural inclination is to try something different. Here's where it gets interesting... how do we know what to do differently?

Often, we make assumptions like, "He or she just didn't hear me." Or: "I wasn't aggressive enough." Or: "I didn't describe certain features."

But what if we didn't make assumptions and instead asked for feedback directly? The dialogue would completely change. For example, a follow-up conversation could play out like this: "Dear potential customer, I noticed after my presentation you didn't buy anything. Why?"

The response could vary.

"I didn't buy the product because I didn't like it." This seems like direct feedback.

The customer didn't like the product, but did they like us? Maybe. That was not the question, but often that's the answer we as speakers and/or presenters hear. We conclude that we personally are somehow undesirable. As a result, when we are speaking, we interpret every facial response, body gesture, and every form of feedback as an "I like you" or "I don't like you" reaction. In this instance, the speaker and the product are the same, and if the audience doesn't like the product, they don't like me, the speaker.

Let's take a different perspective. Let's separate the speaker from the product or service, which we will now call an "opportunity." If you are the spokesperson or brand representative of this opportunity, it is your job or responsibility to showcase it. You are tasked to connect the value of this opportunity to the needs and wants of the customer. It's fair to say you are an expert on this opportunity and, as the expert, you are sharing your knowledge about it with others.

Breaking it down this way, we can better distinguish the difference between our desire for a connection, the value of the opportunity, and our expertise. So, where is our problem? Is it the way we are presenting? No, not entirely.

Often we focus on changing the wrong thing: the speaker. What? "If I am not being an effective communicator—salesman, spokesperson, or brand representative— then certainly 'I' must be the issue."

That's partly true. But we, as speakers, are only part of the communication dynamic. The other equally important part we often overlook is that each of us is also the listener.

Why am I breaking this down now? It has a direct link to *how we show up*. If we see ourselves as only a speaker, our focus is limited. We're trying to "fix" the way we present—with only half the story. It is the surface we try to change.

This leads to self-defeating thinking. I cannot tell you the countless times people have come to me and said, "I am not engaging enough." "I am not interesting enough." "I just need to be more likeable."

Regardless of the comment, they all end with "Help me."

What I can do is help you help yourself.

The real issue here isn't trying to find a way to be more likeable, interesting, or engaging. It is how to create or know the context where you can be your most likable, interesting, and engaging self.

When we get caught up in finding ways to fulfill the way "I need to be or act," we find short-term superficial solutions that are difficult to sustain long-term. This is especially true when we start comparing ourselves to others whom we consider successful. We look at that guy as being "suave and charming" and he always gets the girl. Good for him. That doesn't mean you should try to be like him.

To be a better communicator, become a better listener. We are both speaker and receiver simultaneously in the communication dynamic. We often learn to focus on only one aspect of this dynamic—the speaker. This is why learning external speaking techniques, such as how to appear funny or charming, without fully delving inward, produces a finite exchange.

Remember, it is an inside-out approach. Your personal charisma thrives when you uncover how to be authentic and effective in the communication cycle, regardless of the context.

Let's look at the communication cycle more thoroughly.

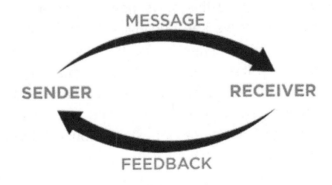

As a sender, you deliver messages to the receiver. In exchange, the receiver sends feedback to you. The exchange is influenced by static (potential obstacles or distractions) and context (the scenario for the exchange and the demographic of the audience). This is the core of every communication dynamic, whether it is a one-on-one conversation or a group presentation.

Here is an example of a group dynamic: a breast cancer survivor (sender/speaker) is giving a ninety-minute keynote presentation (context) to 200 doctors (receiver/audience) about the best practices for approaching cancer patients (message). All of these elements are established beforehand. Feedback occurs in the exchange.

How does one become a better listener and thrive in the communication cycle? It is through two behaviors: (1) active listening and (2) creating distinctions.

Active listening is when you repeat or mirror back the feedback you are receiving. It is a *form of validation*.

For example, your co-worker may be upset with the manager for requiring the team to work on the weekend and say, "I am pissed! It's totally unfair that we had to work on Saturday."

An active listener would respond by saying, "I hear you are frustrated about having to give up your weekend plans or personal time to work on this project. I completely understand your feelings." In this example, the listener plays back and interprets the feedback, as well as empathizes with it.

Validation is a useful tool in the art of active listening. It also allows the receiver (now turned speaker) to offer reciprocal feedback that may further explain the original response in a communication-building fashion. In the example above, the response might continue, "I completely understand your feelings. I was upset, as well, but appreciate having the overtime and feeling of accomplishment."

Here you see the conversation is continuing, which is important in this example because it helps builds the relationship and minimize resentment. There is an exchange of ideas. It doesn't stop with, "I am pissed!"

When conflicts or misunderstanding arise, skills like active listening can help mitigate the damage. Active listening also helps speakers with their presentations. For example, "The last time I spoke on this issue there was some confusion, so I am going to share this diagram. Once I am done explaining it, I am going to leave time for questions."

Here the speaker listened to her previous audience and created some clarifying points.

Another example is when a celebrity tells a behind-the-scenes story about his latest project because his fans love those stories. How does he know? From previous feedback.

Can you think of a few other examples you've seen or experienced where feedback produced a better presentation or interaction?

Creating Distinctions

The second behavior for thriving in the communication cycle is creating distinctions. This is the ability to listen deeply to feedback and offer clarity around an unanswered question or an unexplained idea. It requires respect, descriptive language, and patience.

The sender must be humble enough to realize that his words may need further explanation. So, he chooses to describe what he is talking about in more detail using simple, clear details. Also, the sender has to take the audience response for what it is: a question or need for clarification. He cannot be defensive or take the feedback as a negative opinion on him as a speaker. Ego must not get in the way.

An unanswered question may be hidden in the feedback. Therefore, the sender has to listen for what is being implied or intuit how the receiver may be taking or not taking in the information. For example, in a work situation a supervisor—the sender—may get feedback from an employee—the receiver—such as, "What you are asking us to do is impossible."

What does this feedback really mean? It might mean the receiver is scared, concerned or stressed. Here, the supervisor is challenged not to react to the feedback as mere pushback for the sake of not doing the work. If the supervisor wants to communicate more effectively, then he or she should probe further.

A potential response might be, "I realize this task may seem very daunting, so I'd like to offer some support. What do you need?"

With this type of response, the communication continues.

Distinctions are also needed in the questions we ask. For example, earlier when the salesman asked for feedback from his audience in this fashion, "Why don't you like the product?" he might have asked a better question: "What information can I give you about this product that would be useful to you?" Or, he might have said: "What can we do to make this product more useful? I will take the information back to my supervisors."

This extra step is a trust-building response... and while this is a sales example, the same probing can be equally effective in personal relationships. Imagine hearing from a spouse during a disagreement, "What can I do to make this situation better now and in the future?"

Let's look at the skills of active listening and creating distinctions in communication a little more in depth with two examples.

The Entertainer and the Nurse

I've had the privilege to interview a few celebrities more than once, and most are gracious and wonderful. Part of the reason I believe this to be true is that they are willing to speak to the Press when needed. They appreciate their audiences.

The entertainer was no exception. As an Emmy- Grammy- Oscar- and Tony-award winning performer, you would suspect she might not be that accessible. But she was truly down-to-earth and seemed to love her job as a personality. At least, that's the impression she gave me.

She knew how to work her audience—whether it was on stage, on set, or in an interview setting one-on-one. She also knew how to work the interviewer to get the most out of the exchange. Sometimes interviewers go through the motions of their job without much care about how well it is done. While that wasn't the case with me, she did everything she could to get great feedback from me and, in return, gave me and the audience I represented a good interview.

Not an on-camera interviewer, I usually sat next to the camera, opposite the celebrity. Once, however, she shook things up and pulled me in front of the camera. "For all of you out there wondering who I am talking to, it's this guy with the spiked hair. I am not talking to myself! Maybe it's because of his hair that he stays off camera."

It was a funny moment that got me on my feet, both literally and figuratively. I laughed and played along with her, going back and forth between being sender and receiver. Her natural and charming charisma—witty, engaged, and sincere—came across every time I interviewed her.

This entertainer was Whoopi Goldberg.

My experience with Whoopi serves as a great example of the communication cycle in action. We both offered feedback that helped build the conversation. It was not an interview that looked like a tennis match, where the ball went back and forth in the form of question then answer, then question and answer again. The interview resembled a dance, where we moved fluidly on the dance floor, in unison. I feel the dance metaphor is the perfect way to describe the communication cycle operating at its best.

Another example of mastering feedback in the communication cycle is Nurse Barb. She is a nurse practitioner, product spokesperson, and local TV personality in the U.S. I first started working with her as a media coach, preparing her for press interviews. Later I helped develop and package her as a personality brand. My business partner, Adora English and I took Nurse Barb's on-camera skills and ability to create online content and began marketing her as a brand ambassador for pharmaceutical companies and over-the-counter products.

As a nurse practitioner specializing in women's health, she is a natural detective. Her job is to get to the source of potential health concerns. When patients come into her office, she interviews them. She has to dig deep as an active listener, often validating her patients' experiences. For example, she says, "I understand that must be stressful and you are concerned..." This is followed up by, "What I am hearing you say is..."

This also calls her to create very clear distinctions. When someone says they are in pain, she asks if it is an ache, soreness, tension, throbbing, or a sharp, knife-cutting feeling.

These skills—active listening and creating distinctions— which Nurse Barb developed over time, have helped equip her to be a good speaker. They have also helped her be charismatic on camera as a brand spokesperson. She comes across as friendly, kind, and informative.

Similarly, we each possess a detective nature that can assist with our active listening skills. Being able to dance in the communication cycle helps us utilize and sharpen our charisma.

Whoopi Goldberg goes between sender and receiver with ease and, as a result, draws in audiences with her wit and humor. In Nurse Barb's case, her active listening skills and ability to create distinctions showcase her helpful and nurturing nature.

Lesson Learned

Good listeners make for better communicators

In the communication cycle, flowing between sender and receiver and active listening is essential for charisma. Why? Because it opens us up and helps free us from perceived notions on how to speak.

Summary

- How you thrive within the communication cycle as both sender and receiver helps your authentic charisma flow naturally.
- To be a better speaker, or sender, requires being a better listener.
- Two ways to become a better listener are through active listening—paraphrasing with empathy and understanding—and creating distinctions in language and explanations.
- Communication is not a tennis match, where questions go back and forth; it is more of a dance.

Exercise

1. Think about the last big conflict or argument you had with someone.

2. When you replay the conversation, do you hear any sentiments that weren't directly said such as, "You were wrong." Or "I was right."

3. Were there any thoughts you didn't adequately express, such as "I see your point," or "I understand you."

4. How could you have expressed yourself differently? How could you have listened differently? What assumptions were made?

The Call to Action

Challenge yourself in your next argument to really hear someone out, validate his or her experience, and engage in a solution. *__You are both the sender and the receiver in a conversation.__* Even if all you want to do is make a point, you have to make sure you are being heard. This means to listen to feedback.

CHAPTER 13

Charisma in Communication Tool Kit

Five Tips for Tapping into Charisma

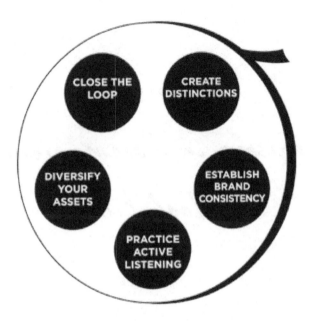

Charisma is unleashed when we get out of our own way and allow our best selves to step forward. Here are some ways to tap into your natural charisma in the same way that high-profile figures prepare for press interviews and public appearances.

Tapping into Charisma *Tip #1: Create Distinctions*

Paint a picture with your words. Use descriptive language that truly describes the details and essence of your message. Avoid over-summarizing. Don't use industry-specific language or lingo. Explain jargon and acronyms. Technical terms that are familiar with one of your audiences may be unfamiliar to another.

Make sure when people hear a word you use that they know what it means. If it takes a few more words in order to be more specific, that's ok. For example, saying "I like fruit" is different from saying, "Apples are the nectar of life." Be purposeful and definitive in what you say. Don't tell people you are funny; share a funny story that shows your humor. Don't tell an audience that you are sassy and sophisticated; show them through powerful, well-crafted, sassy, and sophisticated messages.

Tapping into Charisma Tip #2: Establish Brand Consistency

Audiences want something real that they can rely on again and again. When you speak or present yourself to others, what are they expecting to see and hear? Branding is how you connect emotionally to your audience, sustain their trust, and remain accountable to them. It is the promise you make that distinguishes you and your offer. Therefore, it is important to take time to define and refine what sets you apart. Being consistent and committed to the brand creates fans that are loyal and supportive.

Tapping into Charisma Tip #3: Practice Active Listening

Listen to what is *not* being said. There is so much more to hear than just the words being spoken to you. Sometimes others feel they are clear with their message, but they are not. You may have to investigate assumptions of understanding, feelings, and thoughts not verbally expressed. Sometimes you can use your intuition, but even that requires feedback.

A simple practice is to repeat back to the other person what you've heard. You can also ask questions. It is far better to check in with someone, even if it's annoying to him or her, than it is to make assumptions of understanding that can lead to bigger problems. Often, even in the closest of relationships, we need to practice our active listening skills.

Tapping into Charisma Tip #4: Diversify Your Assets

Most people think that energy means speaking rapidly at a high volume, sentence after sentence. Let's get it straight right now—that's annoying. Nobody wants to hear someone do that. It's exhausting. Energy means having highs and lows in volume and pace. The more you practice or try different tactics, like using the power of silence in certain moments, or sharing a compelling story, the more diverse you can be in your communication. The trick is to practice your diverse assets when the stakes are safe, so it will be more natural to do when the stakes are high.

Tapping into Charisma Tip #5: Close the Loop

Unanswered questions are the worst. They leave us feeling annoyed, unappreciated, or ignored. Plus, without a clear response, we assume the answer—and often in a negative way.

A simple answer like "yes" or "no" shows respect and decisiveness. Even an undecided answer, like "I am taking this into consideration," shows that you honor the request. Answering questions, following up on outstanding requests, and saying "thank you" all create clarity and show respect. That is charisma in action. You pull people toward you versus shutting them out.

SECTION VI:

Celebrity Quotient

CHAPTER 14

Celebrity Quotient

Celebrity Branding Principle: **You design, develop, and manage the way you want to come across through a tool called your Celebrity Quotient (CQ).**

Being a star requires work. There is no easy way to say it. The good news is that the skills to be a star already exist within you.

Now that we've explored the 3Cs, it's time to connect the dots further. Your *star quality* can be packaged through a tool I've developed called your *Celebrity Quotient*—your *CQ*.

What is CQ?

CQ is the measure of your celebrity essence as designed, developed and managed by you. It is a way to track and maintain the way you want to come across—the impact you want to make with your audience. It shows up as your charisma and lays the foundation for your personal brand.

For example, someone might want to come across as powerful, compassionate, and loving, while another person may want to come across as sexy, deliberate, and funny. Each one of these personas is distinct. They each look, feel, and sound different.

They each have a distinct and *unique value proposition* (UVP).

A person we envision as powerful, compassionate, and loving is different from a person we see as sexy, deliberate, and funny. They are two different people, two different products, two different personality brands.

By identifying the characteristics or the impression we want to make and how we want others to receive us, we lay the foundation for communicating and self-promoting our best selves. This determines the language we use, the pace of our wording, how we dress, eye contact and more. Basically our *CQ* establishes our communication *style*. An individual who is powerful, compassionate, and loving uses different words,

165

dresses differently, commands different eye contact, and delivers his or her words differently than someone who identifies as sexy, deliberate, and funny.

In the example above, we are looking at two very different creatures. Think of one as a *purple polka-dotted zebra* and the other as a *rainbow checkered penguin*. Both are special and unique. Both are attractive. Both are wildly provocative. Yet, each is a special being with distinct characteristics. They move, show up, and communicate differently.

We are like those creatures. Personally, I love penguins, but I am definitely more like a purple polka-dotted zebra.

How to Use CQ

CQ is a road map for communication delivery and engagement. It informs our actions, what to wear, what to say, how to say it, and in what circumstances. It is a pledge to our personal brand. It starts with identifying characteristics that authentically and powerfully describe our "best self." It helps determine and shape what kind of everyday celebrity we want to be.

I developed the *CQ* tool by observing celebrities over the past few decades. Do they use this same measure? Yes, but not as consciously as I have described. They have a team of people around them who help guide their image and identify their personal brands.

For example, the message and image are different when an R&B ballad singer talks about a romantic interlude than when a country singer talks about suffering or a dance pop star talks about hooking up with someone. There is a difference between a leading lady who always has to be charming and a comedic sidekick who always has to be funny. So, the team around a celebrity helps define what makes that star unique and valuable.

Establishing your *CQ* is actually quite simple. All you have to do is identify three characteristics you like about your best self that you want to convey to others.

Take a look at and isolate the desired impression you want to make. Once you've created a personality profile from these three characteristics, such as "inspiring, passionate, and smart," think about personal stories, natural gestures, language, and the authentic mindset needed to achieve this personality brand.

Identifying your *CQ* can help create better communication dynamics, leadership skills, and relationships. It also builds your inner confidence that can help you feel more fulfilled, knowing that you've touched your higher purpose.

Award Season and the Leading Lady

CQ is found throughout the entertainment business and here's a story to help exemplify how it organically shows up with minimal effort. Many in the industry say L.A. has two seasons—pilot season and award season. While I personally don't know about piloting, which is creating a sample program of scripted drama or sitcom, I worked in entertainment press and can say with great certainty that award season is like the Super Bowl or World Cup.

On the morning of the Academy Awards Show, a publicist friend of mine described the event on Facebook as "Hell Week." Why? Because behind the scenes everyone—publicists, reporters, entertainment TV hosts, talent agents, managers, and producers—is on high alert.

They are working twenty-seven hours straight to cover red carpet arrivals, the actual award show and the parties afterward. Or they are nervous as hell about the results because a client is either going to win and catapult to a new level of admiration—or lose.

As an entertainment news producer, I used to be in the bunch that worked twenty-seven hours straight. Early in my career, one of my assignments for a local L.A. TV news station was to assist the five o'clock live entertainment morning news report from the site of the Academy Awards—the Oscars. As a production assistant, I was expected to help in any way possible—pull cables from the satellite truck, run to get coffee, hold the reflector which bounced sunlight onto the face of the journalist, write cue cards, assist the camera man and more. Whatever anyone needed, I was there to help.

After the live reports wrapped at 8:25 a.m., I was told to stay. My new assignment was to secure our spot on the red carpet. What did that entail? It meant I had to stand with the camera tripod—without the camera on it—and make sure nobody else encroached on our spot. So for the next seven-and-a-half hours I just stood there.

This, my friends, is the glamour of Hollywood—and I wouldn't trade the experience for anything! As I stood there, I took stake not only in the station's and entertainment reporter's spot on the red carpet, but also my own stake in the *world of celebrity*.

I have many fond memories from not only that first job, but also from the next fifteen-plus years where I had the privilege to be on the red carpet for almost every award show—the Academy Awards, the Grammy Awards, the Primetime Emmy Awards, the Daytime Emmy Awards, the Golden Globes, the People's Choice Awards, the Soul Train Awards, the ESPN's

ESPY Awards, the MTV Video Music Awards, the MTV Movie Awards, the Nickelodeon Kid's Choice Awards, and more. I had the pleasure of working on the red carpet with TV hosts, interviewing celebrities myself, and also working the pressroom with all the winners. I got to know fellow entertainment producers, publicists, reporters, and hosts. We were kind of like a family, traveling from one award show, press conference, backstage interview, and junket to the next.

Why is a spot on the red carpet so important? Placement on the red carpet shows your rank of importance. The closer you are to the door, the more important you are to that award show's organization. It's a status symbol. The spots near the entrance were considered the best because celebrities might bypass the other interviewers in the back of the line. Sometimes stars only stopped once or twice before entering the venue, so you wanted to be near the prime spots just to get footage of them.

In addition to placement on the red carpet, another important factor to getting interviews is relationship capital, which is your reputation and ongoing alliances. As a producer, entertainment reporter, or TV host, you constantly have to be connected to celebrity handlers, namely their publicists, whose jobs are to be gatekeepers of the press.

If you are known as being fair or celebrity-friendly, then you are on the good list. If not, just like Santa's list, you are on the naughty list. Now, of course, it's not this simple because, like all businesses, there are other political factors involved.

Everyone involved, from the camera operator and technician in the satellite truck to the producer and entertainment reporter behind the velvet rope, to the celebrity with his or her publicist on the red carpet, knows this is a business. It is the business of promotion—and more specifically, self-promotion.

Even though it rarely rains in Los Angeles, it almost always rains on at least one award show, if not more, per award season. One particular year, over a decade after my very first show, was no different.

It was the People's Choice Awards and it was being done at a smaller venue, just outside of Los Angeles. The star power was still impressive.

After a day of interviewing some fascinating celebrities, it was time to strike the crew and wrap. This means to break down the lights, put away the cables, and pack up because the shoot is over. This process can take an hour or more, depending on the size of the crew. The other crews had pulled their equipment together and gone into the pressroom. Working for a smaller entertainment channel at the time, we were at the end of the press line and did not even have access to the backstage pressroom.

It was quiet, cool, and chilly. The front of the auditorium was pretty empty by then and a publicist came running down the stairs. She whisked right past us and approached a limo that had just pulled up. The car door opened and out stepped one of the most beautiful leading ladies I've ever seen. The publicist greeted her and they started to walk up the stairs.

As they walked, I turned to my fellow producer and friend, Shahnti, and said, "Do you think that is…" and she said, "Yes." We called her name and asked, almost pleading with her, "Can we chat with you?"

It seemed like the longest pause in history.

She turned around, glanced at us, smiled, and then came forward. Normally, when celebrities come that late they are sneaking in to avoid the press. Knowing the game, value of promotion, and appreciating that this is part of her job, she gave us a non-verbal "Yes."

I don't really remember what we even asked her. Shahnti may remember, but in front of us was a celebrity who was very selective with her interviews and we asked a pretty lame question. Something like, "How does it feel to be here tonight?"

She gracefully answered the question, and then kindly gave us a "Is there more?" type of glance. The constant professional, she said, "Thank you" and looked at us one more time with her unique megawatt smile. As she walked into the auditorium, I knew that would be one of the few professional opportunities I would ever have to speak with Julia Roberts.

I felt as though once again I had come in contact with celebrity royalty. That exchange reminded me about two things: (1) a large part of *celebrity essence* is knowing that self-promotion is part of the gig, and (2) when you have the moment to dance in the spotlight with someone—like we did with her—know what you want.

To be honest, as interviewers, our *CQ* was not present. We were not as prepared as we could have been, but the leading lady definitely was prepared and knew her brand. Her *CQ* was present and apparent. She came across as kind, thoughtful, and friendly.

Celebrity Quotient is a tool that gauges charisma. Therefore it is important to know, in advance, how you want to come across. There's a question that helps bring *CQ* to life: "When I walk away, what do I want people to say about me?"

You want them to say something positive and memorable rather than have no opinion at all.

Celebrity Quotient taps into your natural skills and helps you identify and amplify them. You can use those skills for better communication and ultimately better results, either personally or professionally. If you want to be a more effective boss, you can tap into your *Celebrity Quotient* to make sure that you are mobilizing your staff. If you want to make an impression with new people, you can look at your *CQ*. If you want to "work it" on a date, take a look at your *CQ* and whether or not it is truly representing who you are.

Lesson Learned

Be prepared in advance on how you want to be seen

Do we need to have all three of the 3Cs, or can we just have one to be at our best? I believe all three are essential to really foster your personal *celebrity essence*. The good news is you are probably already strong in one or two of the areas and just may not know it. Therefore, you can concentrate on developing the other one(s). Identifying your *CQ* is the guideline that helps you pinpoint what area to concentrate on and how you may or may not be achieving your self-promotion goals.

Celebrity Quotient can be measured. First, take a moment to consider your *CQ*. What three qualities exemplify your best self? How do these qualities show up with clarity, confidence, and charisma? Do they enhance your *celebrity essence*?

Determining your *CQ* is the guideline for fostering your personal brand.

Summary

- Like celebrities, we all live on the stage of public opinion. It is natural to desire respect and admiration.
- *Celebrity Quotient* (*CQ*) taps into your natural *celebrity essence* and amplifies it by isolating three characteristics that showcase your best self.
- Your *CQ* is the foundation for your personal brand.

Exercise

1. List three qualities you want to show others. For example: powerful, smart, and sincere or witty, creative, and visionary. Look at the list below for some suggestions. Do not limit yourself to them. Please personalize and add your own attributes to the list. This is merely a launching point for internal reflection.

2. After you've written down and reflected on three characteristics, give thought to why you've identified these three qualities to showcase your best self.

3. Next, ask two people who know you well to list your top three characteristics. Ask them to describe, without guiding them in a particular direction, how you come across.

4. Then, compare their responses with your own desire. Do they match? Why or why not?

CQ Characteristics

Smart	Clever	Provocative	Funny	Cosmopolitan
Sexy	Authoritative	Approachable	Determined	Compassionate
Kind	Thoughtful	Intelligent	Ambitious	Witty
Sarcastic	Passionate	Inspiring	Friendly	Assertive
Flamboyant	Artistic	Sophisticated	Down to Earth	Elegant
Grounded	Sincere	Trustworthy	Loving	Creative
Empathetic	Commanding	Powerful	Honest	Direct
Candid	Detailed	Considerate	Hot	Animated

The Call to Action

We navigate how we want the world to see and experience us. How do you want to be seen and heard? Make a decision.

CHAPTER 15

Measuring Your CQ

Celebrity Branding Principle: **Being liked is not enough. People need a compelling reason to continue to listen to you.**

We all are stars and can harness our own special *celebrity essence* if we choose to do so. It is now time to dig deep and unearth exactly how to tap into and showcase our extraordinary selves.

You are the master of your *CQ*. You define and refine it as your star continues to shine. But how do you know if you're making the grade? How do you read people's reactions to interpret for yourself whether your *star quality* is shining bright? In this chapter we will look at how to measure *CQ* so that you can adjust what you convey to others in order to maximize the impression you leave them.

Our *CQ* is measured through feedback. Feedback in the *world of celebrity* is very specific. The desired result is to be admired to the point that it translates into record sales, box office sales, or TV ratings. Real tangible numbers that measure success. Feedback such as "I like him" is not enough. It needs to be more specific.

We seldom say we "like" our favorite celebrities. Instead we imply it. We say, "She is so talented, creative, and outspoken." We describe what we like about them—we identify their *CQ*, the qualities that we find most attractive about them.

Adora, my business partner, coined the phrase "Be Bold. Be Heard. Be Admired."

This is definitely true when it comes to your *CQ*. One has to be bold in committing to a personal brand or identity. One has to be heard clearly in order to be valued. One has to be admired in order to produce results. Being seen is not enough. Being "liked" is not enough.

Did you hear what I just said? Being SEEN or LIKED is NOT enough. Yet, many respective clients have come to me and said, "Make me a superstar."

My usual response is: "Ok, what makes you a star? What is

it that you do?"

Then, the exchange continues: "People like me. I am good at a lot of things. What do you want me to do?"

I say, "No, what do YOU want to do?"

Prospective client: "I told you. I want to be a star!"

And, that's about where I tune out. There is nothing bold in that declaration. There is no *irresistible offer* that gives one a compelling reason to listen further or to continue the exchange. They have no *UVP*. It is closed-ended dialogue.

While the desired outcome seems to be clear to the prospective client, to me there is a missing element—*an authentic UVP.*

They want to be a star in what? Is it a star as a media expert who is direct, articulate, and likeable? An actor who is dynamic, sexy, and versatile? A TV host who is passionate, inquisitive, and entertaining?

They need a solid *CQ.*

The same is true of any communication exchange. What is the *irresistible offer* that creates a compelling reason for an audience to give you their time, attention, or admiration? Let's put it another way: what is compelling about you, *your UVP?* Both of these point back to your *CQ.*

What makes people lean in and want to hear you after your internal proclamation, "I am a star"?

Saying you are a star is already understood, so why waste your time trying to prove it? It just is.

Professional, well-respected celebrities know this: they are stars. They are bold, heard, and admired. They are purposeful with their public identity and self-promotion. They are the CEOs of their personal brand.

Celebrities also have key stakeholders who build and help maintain personal brands. These four important stakeholders are identified as the:

(1) Celebrity (brand CEO),
(2) Manager or agent (individual tasked with deal making),
(3) Publicist (individual tasked with reputation-building and public identity)
(4) Fan

In a corporate setting, these individuals would be the:
(1) CEO (Chief Executive Officer),
(2) CFO (Chief Financial Officer),
(3) CMO (Chief Marketing Officer)
(4) Customer

Let's apply this more specifically to you. With your own personal celebrity brand you may think, "Wow, I can't afford all these people," or "Where do I find them?"

You don't need to look far. *You* are all these people. No, you don't have a split personality. But you do have the ability to play these roles for yourself, to ask the questions each of these individuals would ask, and to collectively strategize how to best position your brand.

By assessing your personal celebrity brand from these four distinct viewpoints— the celebrity, manager/agent, publicist, and fan—you can gain a better perspective on how to position yourself and shine through your own self-promotion practices. Becoming a new observer or taking an alternative look at who you are provides you with possibilities that you may not have seen before.

In the Newfield Network coaching school, they call this OAR. It stands for Observer, Action, and Results. This means that if you want different results, change the observer you are first, not the actions. For example, try looking at yourself from a publicist's point of view rather than from a fan's perspective. New possible actions become visible through a *change in perspective*. The point of view of the publicist facilitates different possibilities from that of the fan.

Celebrities prepare for an interview with their publicists and other key stakeholders. They know the messages that need to be conveyed. They are there to sell the product being promoted. Likewise, you can be prepared to know the messages you want to convey to others about you and your "product" or brand.

Now, take a moment to consider the intentions of all four of the celebrity roles in your brand. Here are some questions to consider.

As CEO of your celebrity brand:
- What is my personal brand?
- What is its value in the "marketplace" (at home, in business, in social situations and/or in the community)?
- What is my expertise?
- Have I identified my *irresistible offer*?
- How do I want to come across?

As the manager of your celebrity brand:
- What is the UVP of my personal brand?
- What makes it distinct and irresistible?
- Who else out there in the marketplace is similar to me and how can I get a distinctive edge?
- How am I bold, heard, and admired?
- What actions will produce positive outcomes?

As the publicist of your celebrity brand:
- What three characteristics best describe my offer in a

unique and valuable way?
– What biases do I need to fight against in the public's eye?
– Are there any damaging perspectives out there about me?
– In what media do I truly shine?
– What is my public relations strategy?

As the president of your fan club:
– How much fun do I have in my work and/or developing my brand?
– What do I enjoy about it the most?
– What stories can I share about my experience?
– What personal parts of my brand and/or identity do I want to share with others?
– What's next for my ever-evolving personal brand and me?

Many of us can easily look through the lens of at least one or maybe two of these brand stakeholders. The challenge for us is to look through our personality brand from a more comprehensive and strategic perspective—and that means all four perspectives.

If you look at your personality brand from all the perspectives of the celebrity stakeholders, then you have a broader look at your *celebrity essence*. As a result, the way you communicate your *CQ* more authentically represents who you are. This can lead to more fulfillment, satisfaction, and enrichment.

Feedback, as you know, is one of the ways we measure results. Your *CQ* is directly linked to it. If you've identified the way you want to come across, then actually looking at how you come across is important. Obviously, you can't specifically ask, "Am I coming across as xxx, yyy, zzz every day with every audience?" But you can measure it if you are willing to be open to direct feedback.

Let's look at *CQ* in action.

The Chefs and the Rejection

I facilitate TV boot camps for chefs in Los Angeles. My wonderful colleague and friend, Denise Vivaldo, the best food stylist and culinary producer in the business, and I offer half-day workshops for chefs and culinary professionals who want to learn how to present themselves and their work on TV or online.

Working with Denise on these workshops is always fun because we both enjoy our work and we each bring a unique vantage point: she knows the mechanics of cooking for video, while I know how to craft branded messages. Denise is like your favorite outspoken aunt. You know, the one who is brave enough to say what everyone else is thinking and has an ability to tell a great story, colored with honest opinions and a curse word now and then.

Among our early clients were the chefs from the Ritz-Carlton.

It's not easy to do demos on television. TV demonstrations are quick instructional segments, usually three- to -six-minutes, where an expert walks you through the steps and assembly of a craft, recipe, or project. One of the reasons it is challenging is because it is a "talk and do" action. Often, when we speak, we pay attention only to the message. Conversely, if we are doing a project, we focus only on the action or steps of the project.

Doing both at the same time takes skill and savvy.

During our time with the chefs, we discuss branding and CQ. In a TV market saturated with so many chefs, since cooking shows are huge in the U.S., one has to be ambitious and distinct in order to make a mark. Being likeable is not enough. Standing out requires a specialty and CQ.

For example, one chef we coached was a Filipino chef named Edwin, who is a star in the making. He's destined one day, if he continues to build his craft, to have a TV show. He is attractive, skillful, and approachable with a specialized talent for cooking easy Filipino dishes. Another chef we worked with specialized in low-calorie, healthy dishes for women over fifty. She is a direct, in-your-face yet loving character. She, likewise, has a specialized brand.

All of the chefs we've worked with have something unique. They serve as a great example of CQ and personal branding because it is easy to clearly see their specialties. That's just one part of it, however. The other part is how they present their special recipes and brand on camera: their CQ.

Additionally, they are constantly challenged to speak and do. For the rest of us, the chefs bring to the surface a few questions:

– What is our specialty?

– How do we present our work?

– In what ways are we able to speak and "be" in our brands?

Chefs who are successful in building a brand have consistency. They have dishes their customers or audience come to rely on, such as making a certain ethnic cuisine or use of an ingredient. It takes certain skills to remain consistent with your brand. You have to know what you do well and continue to build on that.

The same is true of us. What expertise do we build our brands upon? How are we consistent? Sometimes we have to decide what we don't want to do in order to stand out. That's why consistency may be challenging, especially when you might be asked to do something you don't want to do, or are handed more requests or demands you simply cannot fulfill. We may be inclined to do them out of our desire to be liked or feel we may risk losing a potential audience. But if we say "yes," we may risk much more: trust and loyalty. Audiences will not be loyal to you if you are not loyal to them.

Standing out means you know what you stand for. Saying "no" is challenging for many of us, especially in some cultures. Yet, one of the things I believe is true is that "no" closes the loop in the communication cycle.

When looked at in this context, "no" is not a rejection, but rather a pass on an offer or opportunity. My challenge to you is how you hear the "no." How many times do we hear it as a rejection of us as individuals? How often do we feel that saying "no" is a negative reflection on our abilities?

I've received the sweetest rejection three times in my career from the same celebrity and each time I've felt so special. Yes, I've actually felt good. It's kind of amazing when you think about it.

As a booker and producer, I was constantly sending out requests for interviews. Normally, such a request goes through a celebrity's publicist. So, when I wanted to interview this particular star, I would email my request to her publicist. Each time I got a lovely letter declining the interview.

While a rejection letter seems like a simple gesture, in the *world of celebrity* and often in corporate America, it's quite unusual to receive that extra special touch. To make my rejections even better, they weren't form letters, or at least it didn't feel like they were because each was different. They all were charming, kind, and gracious. These are the same three characteristics I would attribute to the star behind them: Ms. Dolly Parton.

Why is this story relevant? Because it shows that Dolly Parton and her stakeholders are in control of her *CQ* at all times. She consistently comes across as kind, down-to-earth, and personable. Even in declining the interview, in saying no, she was kind and remained in integrity with her personal brand.

So, too, we can remain true to our own *celebrity essence* and *CQ*. Doing something uncomfortable does not require a compromise of integrity. Being a celebrity means remaining clear, confident, and charismatic.

Measuring CQ

Measuring your *Celebrity Quotient* (*CQ*) is not that difficult. Once you identify three *CQ* characteristics you like about yourself that you want to convey to others, these can then be rated on a scale of one to five, with five being the most effective and one being the least effective. Having a good *CQ* is a collective score of twelve or higher and means you are making the impression you want and should continue to build upon. Anything lower means you need to go back and work on your *celebrity essence* using the 3Cs.

Lesson Learned

You can define and refine your Celebrity Quotient (CQ)

Feedback is important in measuring CQ. Trust is also essential. In coaching people through this process during workshops, participants prepare one-minute talks about themselves, who they are, and what they do. As they prepare for this brief self-introduction, they have to keep in mind the three characteristics they want to convey, their *CQ*.

Without telling the room what those three characteristics are, he or she then does the one-minute presentation. Afterward, the room tries to figure out the three characteristics and judges each attribute on a scale of one to five. If a presenter gets twelve points or higher, then he or she has achieved an acceptable *CQ*. If she does not, then she has to go back and re-work her presentation. The magic is to know your authentic message and the three characteristics that show your best self.

The way to improve your *CQ* is through practice and regular assessments. You can improve your *CQ* by identifying your three characteristics, examining them through the various celebrity stakeholder perspectives as described in this chapter, and then measuring the impression you make via feedback. The trick is to get responses from people you may not know. Friends and family are often biased.

Summary

- Our *CQ*, or *Celebrity Quotient* is measured through feedback. We get feedback in the form of results and responses.
- By assessing your personal celebrity brand through multiple viewpoints, you can get a better perspective on how to position yourself in your own self-promotion practices. Remain true and consistent to your *Celebrity Quotient (CQ)*, even in moments when you have to say no.
- You can measure your *CQ* by rating each of your three desired characteristics on a scale of one to five, with five being the most effective. If you reach a total of 12 points, you are achieving your *CQ* and should continue to foster it. If not, consider going back to the 3Cs and identifying what skills you need to work on to improve your *CQ*.

Exercise

1. Prepare a one-minute introduction about yourself. Focus on one aspect of yourself, such as what you do for a living or a strong belief. While preparing, keep in mind your three *CQ* characteristics.
2. Next, find someone you don't know very well and try out your one-minute introduction. This person could be a friend of a friend, someone in line at the grocery store, or at a cocktail party.

3. Afterward, ask that person to identify three characteristics on how you came across. Do not prompt them with your *CQ*; rather, let them come up with the words.
4. Repeat and try it again with one or two more people and see what happens.

The Call to Action

Speak with purpose and intention. Learn what parts of your story make an impact. Pay attention to the phrases, messages, and ideas that truly capture the essence you want to convey. Test your CQ.

CHAPTER 16

Stepping into the Spotlight

There is one key component that underlies all the concepts and tools discussed in this book. It is a crucial element to communication. It is finding *your voice*.

Fine tuning messages and presentation style are important. Effective communication, self-promotion, and *celebrity essence* need these two skills. Your *CQ*, however, requires more. Its success lies in *finding your voice*.

Your voice is that burning desire inside of you that wants to be shared with the world. It lives pure and without preconceived interpretation. It resonates and fuels us. Yet, often it sits, locked away like a prisoner. It is held captive by the way others have defined us, our own notions of how we need to present ourselves, and societal pressures.

Don't get me wrong. These captivators do serve a purpose. They give us a point of reference and are very real pressures of everyday living, but they can be put into context. They do not have to rule or limit our voice.

We have a choice. The choice is an inside-out journey where you find your voice and share it with the world.

Our voice is different from our message. Think of it in terms of hearing versus listening. You can hear someone speak, interpret, and respond accordingly. You know what he or she is trying to convey in terms of words and messages. Take a look at these examples:

"I would like you to pay more attention to me."

"I want to sell you this product."

"Join me next Tuesday at this social event."

All of these notions can be heard and responded to by the listener. Beyond these messages is a voice inside. It is a voice asking for something that is not said. In the examples above it can be experienced as:

"I want to be valued."

"I have an *irresistible offer.*"

"I want to spend time with you."

They all speak to a very real emotion and human experience. I call this **the higher value**.

A higher value in communication is that emotion, connection, or human desire you wish to convey and share with another person or group. Our voices are made up of higher values. For example, a parent-teacher organization that does fundraising for classroom supplies appreciates the importance of an education, but the higher value is the future of their families, their community, and their world.

At the root of all true and authentic voices lies something deeply personal and important; it is the higher value. Throughout this book, the message has been that you are a remarkable and extraordinary individual.

You being anything less—dimming your light and discounting your *celebrity essence*—is a choice to silence your voice.

You being bold—shining in the spotlight and fostering your authentic self—is a choice to let your voice be heard.

You have opportunities to shine. Seize them.

During a business meeting you have an opportunity to share your personal contributions to the company. During a date, you have an opportunity to share intimate experiences, and during an argument, you have an opportunity to share your deep conviction and passion.

The Evolving You

These three elements—your CQ, personal brand, and your voice—make the complete package of you. But they are not set in stone forever. Your *CQ* can change. As you grow, you may tweak it because your personal brand has evolved. As you experience new wonders and growth, your voice also continues to shape, morph, and build.

Many people—both well-known personalities and everyday celebrities—have been able to successfully reinvent themselves again and again. I admire those who are brave enough to evolve their personal brands in an authentic and genuine way, and that is my hope for you. Don't stop.

Claim the Spotlight

Challenge yourself to experience what it means to be a star. Shine in all areas of your life: at work, at home, with friends, in the community, and beyond. Make a choice and commitment to be your exceptional, authentic self. Tell your story.

You Are the Star: Shine Every Day, Everywhere, with Everyone

Celebrity branding may seem simple, but it is not easy. You have to commit to your *celebrity essence* daily. It's an evolving process, one with awesome potential. You are worth the effort.

You see, if you are not in control of your message, someone else will be. Do not let your voice be overshadowed by what others assign to you. Do not dim your light because of societal pressures. Let your extraordinary self, your best self, your *authentic* self, illuminate.

In the end, it's not a question of whether or not you're a star. You *are* a star. It's a question of whether or not you choose to shine.

SECTION VII:

Quick Reference Guides

Your Challenge

Take the tools outlined in this book and apply them to your daily life to become the *Everyday Celebrity* you were meant to be. Continue building your own celebrity story, both in this book and in your life.

Be deliberate in showcasing your best self by practicing the *Art of Authentic Self-Promotion.* It is a process that will take time to develop, just like starting a new exercise program, but it is well worth the effort.

Be patient and persevere. Don't let fear or anxiety keep you from being self-revealing. The next time you are called to step into the spotlight – whether it is to self-promote, pitch, argue, react, meet, connect, or otherwise verbally engage another person or group—remember to ask yourself two important questions:

1. What is **The A Factor** *(Art of Authentic Self-Promotion)?*
2. What is my *CQ (Celebrity Quotient)?*

Use these two tools to ground your communication thinking. Simultaneously, be aware of your delivery.

- Do you embody and show up with *powerful presence?*
- Do you have the 3Cs: clarity, confidence, and charisma?
- Do you own your *celebrity essence?*

Consider a few of the ideas and themes that have been laid out and repeated throughout this book. Let them resonate in you and allow them to soak in.

#Value   #Connection   #Commitment   #Authenticity
#Context   #Consistency   #Engagement   #Respect

The following summaries encapsulate the practices, thoughts, and ideas of the *Everyday Celebrity* and offer at-a-glance guidance:

- **12 Celebrity Branding Principles**
- **Six Key Celebrity Branding Terms**
- **Celebrity Branding Flow Chart**

Use them. It is time to shine. It is time be seen. It is time to be an ***Everyday Celebrity.***

12 Celebrity Branding Principles

Put the power of authentic self-promotion practices to work in your life.

- **Principle 1**: The *world of celebrity* is fueled by self-promotion. Superstars show the world what they want others to see.

- **Principle 2**: We are all celebrities. Yes, every single one of us.

- **Principle 3**: Being a star is not a state of mind; it's a way of being.

- **Principle 4**: *Celebrity essence* is the embodiment of a unique *powerful presence*.

- **Principle 5**: Shift your internal dialogue and witness yourself with clarity.

- **Principle 6**: The key to unlocking powerful self-promotion lies within your ability to navigate between the audience, your agenda, and call to action. This is *The A Factor*.

- **Principle 7**: There are two types of confidence: (1) belief in the value of your message and (2) the "you" that shows up in front of others.

- **Principle 8**: Confidence shows up when you use your entire being and body as a tool of self-expression.

- **Principle 9**: Charisma is the ability to fully engage an audience with your unique and authentic being.

- **Principle 10**: Contextual communication is the most effective form of communication.

- **Principle 11**: You design, develop, and manage the way you want to come across through a tool called your *Celebrity Quotient(CQ)*.

- **Principle 12**: Being liked is not enough. People need a compelling reason to continue to listen to you.

Six Key Celebrity Branding Terms

Celebrity Essence: the awareness of your star power and the choice to be purposeful and strategic with your public identity. It is the ability to select what to reveal about yourself, how to show it, and in what circumstances. You are a celebrity with an exceptional offer that is often called into the spotlight.

Irresistible Offer: a distinct and unique opportunity that comes from your truest and most extraordinary place of being. It is when we tap into something truly authentic in ourselves that is irresistible to others.

The Art of Authentic Self-Promotion (The A Factor): the ability to communicate something exceptional about you and your *irresistible offer*. It is tailored to those who need to hear your message: to directly position yourself with clarity to a specific audience.

Powerful Presence: the strength to show up as your best self. It is the physical manifestation of true confidence. It is when your body shows up exactly as it needs to in that moment with your internal and external energies aligned together.

Alignment Opportunities: instances in which you find common ground, shared experiences, and similar interests with others. They are key elements to building relationships. It requires that you share a little something about yourself.

CQ (Celebrity Quotient): the measure of your *celebrity essence* as designed, developed, and managed by you. It starts with identifying three characteristics that authentically and powerfully describe your best self—and tracks and maintains the way you want to come across to your audience.

Celebrity Branding Flow Chart

BEING A STAR

Exists already. No work required.

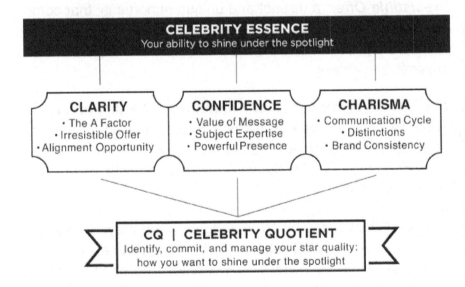

CELEBRITY ESSENCE
Your ability to shine under the spotlight

CLARITY	**CONFIDENCE**	**CHARISMA**
• The A Factor	• Value of Message	• Communication Cycle
• Irresistible Offer	• Subject Expertise	• Distinctions
• Alignment Opportunity	• Powerful Presence	• Brand Consistency

CQ | CELEBRITY QUOTIENT
Identify, commit, and manage your star quality:
how you want to shine under the spotlight

Author's Note

My journey started on a grade school playground. Little did I know then the lasting impact those eighth graders would have on me. I am grateful to them for challenging me to look at how I spoke... and ultimately influencing how I showed up. That early turning point set me on my amazing course.

As a young man, I immersed myself into the world of celebrity media. As a result, I've had the pleasure to meet actors, musicians, TV hosts, media experts, presidents, Nobel Peace Prize winners, executives, speakers, and countless others. It has been a humbling experience. I've conducted the very first interviews with young actors who later went on to win awards, coached performers who sold platinum albums, and trained experts who have gone on to give keynotes in front of thousands.

Yet, among all these experiences, the most rewarding work I've done has been in rooms with everyday celebrities just like you.

Growing up in my small L.A. suburb, I never imagined in my wildest dreams that one day I would work in places like Taipei, Hong Kong, and China. Nor could I have foreseen the type of work that I have been blessed to do on this planet. From the entertainment business in L.A. to the rich culture in Asia, it's all been a privilege.

My entry into the global market has been largely possible because of international business leadership consultant and performance coach Emily Liu. Through a chance meeting at a coaching conference in Colorado, we ended up working together across continents.

Even though each of us has played in different arenas—I in the world of entertainment, media, and communication and Emily in the domain of corporate Asia, leadership development, and performance coaching—together we have created a platform where people can discover and unleash their own individual *star power.* We share with others through workshops, coaching, and now in writing. This book was first published in Mandarin and now in English. To me, that's wild and exciting.

I have witnessed the power of *authenticity in action.* It doesn't matter where you live, how much money you have, your cultural upbringing, or education—you can shine from within. There is a shining unique you waiting, longing, and eager to be seen.

My goal is to make my hands-on experience in Hollywood, throughout the U.S. and in Asia accessible, practical, and useful. I want to instill confidence in what people believe and say about themselves.

This "small brown boy from Azusa," as I often referred to myself, longs to share with others what I've learned in hopes that I can motivate, move, and inspire someone, somewhere along the way.

Author
Jess Ponce III

Jess Ponce III is a personal branding expert, media coach, consultant, speaker, and author.

He is co-founder of Media 2x3, a U.S.-based media company that develops personality brands and manages media opportunities, corporate partnerships, and speaking engagements for a diverse roster of talent

Jess coaches creative and corporate executives, TEDx speakers, professionals, and on-air talent throughout the U.S. Some of his clients include Disney, HGTV, ABC, and other entertainment brands.

A highly regarded international go-to expert on effective communication and personal branding, Jess works internationally in Taipei, Hong Kong, and mainland China in partnership with AsiaWorks.

Jess developed a unique methodology, *The A Factor,* to

teach individuals how to tap into the art of authentic self-promotion. He has worked behind the scenes with countless celebrities and on-air presenters and combines two decades of television experience with networks like E! Entertainment and TV Guide Channel with training from Newfield Network Coach Training to foster the *Everyday Celebrity* in and out of Hollywood.

Whether it is in front of a room, online, in a book, or in front of the camera, Jess Ponce helps individuals develop their personal brand and shine.

Contributor
Emily Liu

Emily Liu is an accomplished entrepreneur, business consultant, executive performance coach, speaker, and author.

In 1986, she introduced human-potential development work from North America to the greater China market. A Taiwan native, Emily is proficient in Chinese and English, and is passionate about innovating, expanding, and elevating experiential learning platforms throughout Asia.

She is the founder and principle consultant of the "awesome GROUP," a multi-platform personal and professional development company. Her organization ignites commitment, power, and action in individuals and teams through books, workshops, videos, and multi-media outlets.

Emily is the author of *Singing in the Rain* and co-author of *Secrets to Winning*, both of which are available in Chinese and English. She is also co-author of the Chinese version of

Everyday Celebrity and a contributor to the English version. She also has co-designed several workshops including: "Secrets to Winning," "Well of Wealth," "Superstar Communication," "Leadership Presence," and "Power of Influence."

She is committed to making transformative changes in the landscape of personal development worldwide. Based in Hong Kong, she travels the globe in the pursuit of this mission.

Acknowledgments

This book has been a labor of love. I've poured myself into it, and with that, many people have helped shape my passion, mission, and work in this world. I am so grateful to them all.

Thank you, Grandma Grace. You were one of my first and best friends as a child and continue to be a lifelong role model.

And to Grandpa Ray, Grandma Rona, Nina Sylvia, Nino Ray, and Aunt Anna, thank you for pushing and inspiring me. Your memories live on.

Family is one of the greatest gifts I've even known. Thank you all of my extended relatives, especially Rosie Garcia, my cousin, who gave me my first break in the entertainment business.

Thank you to Joel Tator and Mark Sonnenberg for taking a chance on a newbie, as well as other professionals who guided me along the way—Gail Nesbit, Gayle Allen, David Salinger and Ramey Warren.

I am also honored to have worked side by side with some amazing colleagues turned friends, especially Shahnti Olcese Brook. We make a great team.

As an author I've received incredible support and encouragement, especially from Liz Jennings, who inspired me to become an indi-author and Sylvia Mendoza, my editor extraordinaire and mentor. Thank you for helping me take the leap. I did it!

I am grateful to those who help me behind the scenes as an author and entrepreneur, including Robin Blakely, Nora Frankovich, Debra Litrov, Jeanie Dobbs, Cindy Jackson, Jen Brookman, and Janell Harris.

To my friends Rob Gilbert, Michael Stevens (deceased), Loren Ruch, Jered Gold, Tim Curtis, Jill Bandemer, Sharon Hashimoto, Ben Sullivan, Tricia Uneda, Jeanine Persell, and Erik Persell; I really appreciate your love and support through the years.

A special shout out to my friend and confidant, Eleanor Chicolo, who has held my hand through many things, including this book—you keep me grounded in so many ways.

To great clients like Nurse Barb Dehn and Dr. Deborah Gilboa (aka Dr. G); your trust helps me and others shine. It's people like you who make my work worthwhile.

For the wonderful opportunity to share my work in Taiwan and beyond, I am forever grateful to Linda Lu, the General Manager of AsiaWorks Taiwan.

To my U.S. business partner, Adora English, you are my trusted friend, colleague, and confidant. There is no one I'd rather share the ride with than you.

To my counterpart in Asia and book contributor, Emily Liu—you opened up my world to amazing new experiences. The work we do together is fun, affirming, and at times draining, but always 100 percent fulfilling.

To Spike, you are more than a furry bundle of love—you've been there with me through thick and thin.

To John and Heny Bilemdjian, who genuinely embrace me like a son; Diana Bilemdjian, my second sister and dear friend; Jason Lachenmyer, my cousin who feels more like a little brother; and to my big sister, Antoinette Ponce, who helped a little boy think one day "he could." Your encouragement and support are amazing.

To my Dad and Mom, Jesse and Patricia Ponce—I am eternally grateful. You let me simply be: to climb, to stumble, to find my own way. That freedom was the best gift you could ever give me.

And to my love, Zachary Bilemdjian—thank you for all you do. You see in me what I sometimes cannot see myself. When I don't believe it, you know with certainty I can do better and be better.

Last, and certainly not least—to you, the everyday celebrity. You constantly teach, inform, and inspire me. Please let your authentic self shine. The world needs *you*.

Testimonials

"I've never thought that my ordinary appearance and background, which seem to be a disadvantage to me, would become my biggest advantage in inspiring others. After Jess Ponce's coaching, I had a deeper conversation with myself, embraced myself and became clear on the value that I deliver to people."

Lin Yu Chun, (Jimmy),
International singer, actor

*

"Jess is a shining star who inspires countless celebrities, experts, and real people. I have personally benefitted from his coaching, and have also seen the benefits of his coaching on clients of mine who I've sent his way. He has helped numerous of our talent discover their own voices, their own charisma, and their own star qualities. As a result, we have confident, dynamic, and creative hosts who are celebrated by millions of viewers each week."

Loren Ruch,
*Vice President of Programming, Partnerships and Special Events
Home & Garden TV (HGTV), DIY Network*

*

"My life and business is more fulfilling and successful because Jess Ponce has been my media and personal coach for years. His insights, experience, warmth, humor, and endless stream of advice and tips have helped me be perfectly prepared for every opportunity and brought me places I never dreamed of."

Nurse Barb Dehn,
On-Air Medical Personality
www.nursebarb.com

*

"Each consecutive day I watched our talent improve as result of Jess's coaching. They liked him, trusted him, allowed themselves to be vulnerable with him, and most of all -- they implemented what they learned from him."

David Salinger,
Vice President Programming
KGO-TV / ABC San Francisco

*

"Jess Ponce gives us the permission to step out of our little mind-prison and into a world where we shine like the bright lights we are. He reminds us to embrace our power and step onto a larger stage than the office or living room."

Adora English,
Partner, Media 2x3

*

"Within 30 seconds, Jess can spot the learning key point for each person... and it's so practical and useful."

Linda Lu,
*AsiaWorks Taiwan Board Member
and General Manager*

*

"This book is a "must have" for anyone dealing with business relationships and everyday interpersonal relationships. You will be touched by Jess's anecdotal stories and be challenged by his questions at the end of each chapter. If you struggle with how to bring out the best in yourself and your talents, you need to have this book on your desk for everyday use."

Eleanor Chicolo,
(Retired) Executive, Visa

Made in the USA
Las Vegas, NV
14 May 2022

48886930R00125